Freedom for the
God-designed Writer In You

# Heather Greer

Copyright © 2025 by Heather Greer

Published by ScrivCraft,
an imprint of Scrivenings Press LLC
15 Lucky Lane
Morrilton, Arkansas 72110
https://ScriveningsPress.com

Printed in the United States of America

All rights reserved. No part of this publication may be reproduced, stored in a retrieval system, or transmitted in any form or by any means—for example, electronic, photocopy, and recording— without the prior written permission of the publisher. The only exception is brief quotations in printed reviews.

Paperback ISBN 978-1-64917-462-8

eBook ISBN 978-1-64917-463-5

Editor: Linda Fulkerson

Cover design by Linda Fulkerson - www.bookmarketinggraphics.com

Scripture quotations are taken from the New American Standard Bible® (NASB), Copyright © 1960, 1962, 1963, 1968, 1971, 1972, 1973, 1975, 1977, 1995 by The Lockman Foundation. Used by permission.

NO AI TRAINING: Without in any way limiting the author's [and publisher's] exclusive rights under copyright, any use of this publication to "train" generative artificial intelligence (AI) technologies to generate text is expressly prohibited. The author reserves all rights to license uses of this work for generative AI training and development of machine learning language models.

*To the frustrated and discouraged writers who question their path every time they fail. I've been there. Know that God sees you. God understands you. And the way He designed you is not a mistake, even if it feels that way sometimes.*

# CONTENTS

| | |
|---|---|
| *Introduction* | vii |
| 1. My Own Special Blend | 1 |
| 2. Good to the Last Drop | 7 |
| 3. Mixing It Up for a Perfect Blend | 15 |
| 4. Your Writing World | 25 |
| 5. No Time Like the Present | 37 |
| 6. Taking Responsibility | 45 |
| 7. Christian Writers Write Christian Content | 51 |
| 8. Write What You Know | 61 |
| 9. Plotters, Pantsers, and Plantsers ... Oh, My! | 71 |
| 10. Getting the Words Out | 81 |
| 11. Creating Convincing Characters | 87 |
| 12. Traditional or Not at All | 95 |
| 13. Moving Forward | 107 |
| *Additional Resources* | 111 |
| *Acknowledgments* | 113 |
| *About the Author* | 115 |
| *Other Writing Craft Books You May Like* | 117 |
| *Also by Heather Greer* | 121 |

# INTRODUCTION

My Writing Life is Over Before It Begins

My writing dreams couldn't end like this.

I sat in yet another writer's conference as published authors, the authorities on writing well, touted a need to plot out every detail of my stories to make them stronger. The message was consistent with what I'd heard at my previous conference and the one before that.

According to what everyone taught, good writing required intense pre-planning. Every detail from plot points to a character's backstory should be accounted for before writing the first word of the first paragraph. The system was very structured, very detailed, and so very *not* like me.

I desired to be a strong writer—more than anything. God placed in my heart a passion for story. Every imagination and emotion-capturing story I'd ever read confirmed in me the need to create my own. I'd prayed about my path and moved forward, convinced in my heart that writing faith-based fiction was God's plan, prepared for me before I was even born.

I tried incorporating the lessons learned at the feet of these writing masters. They instructed me on the steps leading to author

## Introduction

success. Harnessing their ways would allow me to craft stories readers would return to again and again. It had to be true. These were known authors in the Christian publishing industry. If I diligently followed their path, I would enjoy the same success.

I tried.

I failed.

Again and again, I tried.

Each time I failed.

Character development sheets sat on my desk only partially filled in. Major plot points escaped my synopsis. Every time I tried following those step-by-step instructions, my stories stalled. I struggled to get my words on the page. The story that once flowed with a rhythm worthy of dance, now crept along at an impossibly slow pace.

With discouragement weighing me down, I attended one more conference. This one was different. It was small, intimate. Registrations were limited to a handful. I wasn't sure what to expect, except for more of the same message I'd heard so many times before.

Even with the certainty of more discouragement waiting for me, I looked forward to the gathering for one reason. My favorite author was presenting. Her participation prompted my husband to register me for the conference as an anniversary gift. Meeting my favorite author gave me something to look forward to, a bright spot to ease the weight of my discouragement. Whether I ever wrote another word or not, missing the opportunity to meet her was not an option.

My assumptions about the presentations were correct. The message remained true to what I'd heard before: Plot. Plot. And plot some more. I gleaned nuggets of wisdom from each speaker. As authors who excelled in their craft, there was much to learn from them. And maybe, hopefully, this time, the plotting lessons would stick.

Then, she rose to speak.

"I'm going to say something different from what you've already heard. I'm not a plotter, and that's okay."

*Introduction*

I can't confirm these as her exact words, but it was her message. Hope flamed inside me. My favorite author, the one whose stories fed my imagination and encouraged my soul with their messages of faith, didn't subscribe to the plotter's school of writing. Well-developed characters and strong plotlines filled her pages, and she accomplished it without planning out each step ahead of time. In fact, she admitted to being as surprised as her readers by the things her characters did and said.

Hope nudged open the door to my writer's heart. If she could succeed as an author without sacrificing her writing style, could I accomplish the same? Was this ability unique to her due to some innate talent others did not possess?

Armed with this new encouragement, I moved forward with reserved confidence in my writing. I'd know soon enough if she was an anomaly in the writing world.

But before committing myself to this renewed direction, my dream needed to return to the Dream Giver. I'd been in a serious place of doubt, and I didn't own the dream. It was on loan to me from God, and I couldn't go forward without His blessing even if I was re-energized by the workshop. I prayed. I waited. He confirmed it in me once again.

Time to move forward, though I lacked assurance of what I believed constituted success. God's idea of success for my writing could be different from my own.

Later, God opened my heart to additional truth He'd sown at that conference and cultivated through the years. Though I didn't understand it at the time, there was a scriptural basis for the freedom I felt in hearing I could write well without the confines of the plotter's system. Understanding two key truths, I've embraced who I am as an author and gained confidence in my ability to write stories that will keep readers coming back for more.

I pray these truths will help you too.

# 1

# MY OWN SPECIAL BLEND

You write you. Writing in ways natural to you sounds simple. But if we're also to write well, there are vital steps we can't ignore. The first step in learning to write you, is knowing who *you* are. Without this understanding, none of us can hope to achieve better writing through techniques that complement our natural tendencies.

My coffee-loving children enjoy what they've termed, "blueberry muffin coffee." It's not on any coffee shop menus that I'm aware of, but according to them, if you love coffee, this one is not to be missed. Their special brew is an iced coffee with a splash of hazelnut, a swirl of blueberry, and almond milk. I don't drink coffee, but even I think it sounds like comfort in a cup.

One day, when getting this delightful blend for my child, I had to visit a different coffee shop. I placed my order only to be told they didn't have hazelnut syrup, but they did have a different nutty flavor. My son drank his coffee, but it wasn't the same. One ingredient changed the taste.

The imitation was close. He even admitted it was good. But it wasn't the blueberry muffin coffee he loves.

Even with this blend topping their coffee flavor charts, my kids don't always want it. Sometimes they want something hot or stronger. Sometimes they want plain coffee without the frills.

Whatever they want, one thing remains true: Each drink starts with the same coffee base. The result, however, depends on the added sweeteners, flavorings, creamers, and whether or not ice is added.

I don't enjoy coffee, but there is a sip of truth in this idea, which I appreciate and can employ in my writing as well as many other areas of life. No matter what else is added, we all start with our own personal base.

*"I will give thanks to You, for I am fearfully and wonderfully made; Wonderful are your works, And my soul knows it very well."*
Psalm 139:14, NASB

It's a verse as familiar and comforting as the aroma of freshly brewed coffee. Those who grew up in church have heard it countless times. Sanctity of life month each year? Check. Kids' club and teen youth group meetings? Check. Women's seminars? Check.

Any time people seek encouragement in their God-given worth, Psalm 139:14 is typed onto the slide and added to the presentation. We hear it, claim it, and preach it. But do we stop and think about its ramifications? Do we pay any attention to the last phrase of the verse? Do our souls know very well and live the truths of this verse?

I am fearfully and wonderfully made. I'm not perfect. Far from it. But the Creator of the universe planned and formed me just the way I am.

Science argues that genetics are the cause. There is some truth in the idea. But God created the genetics and orchestrated which DNA from my mother and father would shape my being. He did the same in you.

As a writer, being an introvert is fine. Writing is a solitary endeavor in many ways. Yet, when I am faced with the need to leave the safe haven of my shell for marketing or meeting with editors and agents, I may find this trait less than desirable. Still, it wasn't luck of the draw that wired introversion into my DNA. I can't even blame my father, who is as introverted as I am. None of us can.

We are God's special creation. He mixed our ingredients, not from a prefabricated formula, but individually in the exact amounts He needed present in us. Like my son's blueberry muffin coffee really wasn't the drink he loves without the hazelnut, any of us without even one of our genetic traits would no longer be the individual God created us to be.

God's design only begins with our eye colors and allergies. We're made up of more than our appearances and predispositions to different health issues. Who we are goes deeper than the ailments we struggle with and our natural abilities or lack thereof.

God gifted each of us with personality. Many of our personality traits are hardwired by God into our DNA. The recipe for them is there long before we take our first breath. And God gifted us each trait perfectly for carrying out His plans for us in the way He desires for us to carry them out. Our writing is part of that.

In creating us as the unique individuals we are, God also took into account the events in our lives that would shape us. He knows in advance how each success and failure, hurt and joy, are going to work together with the personality He designed for us. He knows how to use each circumstance and tendency to mold us into the image of Christ and help us live out the dream He's given us in the way we are individually called to do it.

As a Certified LINKED® Personality System Coach, I've always found the unique blend of personality traits individuals possess remarkable. Even two people, sharing the same basic personality types, are still distinct in their ways and wants. Life events, the environment they grew up in, and their relationship with God all play their part. Blended with the biological characteristics, they create a life uniquely theirs and specifically chosen for God's purpose and glory. And they bring the freedom for variation in our writing journeys.

 *You have been thoughtfully crafted to carry out God's purpose for His glory.*

Despite what some believe, knowing your personality doesn't close you into a box of preset actions and reactions. Instead, it gives insight into who and how you are. Inside each personality type and blend, there is a multitude of trait combinations. Just because perfectionism is added to the list of general traits for your personality, you don't have to exhibit that trait. Perhaps you never exhibited that tendency. Or maybe, you recognized it in yourself a long time ago and learned how to let God mold it into the more positive qualities of attention to detail and quality without the overpowering drive for your work or that of others to be perfect.

Even if a trait is seen as positive, it's not guaranteed your unique blend will include that specific one. You are not a generic cup of coffee. You're a specialty drink, mixed with precision by God. Learning about your personality type isn't meant to shape you into the likeness of every other person with the same personality type. It's meant to provide understanding; to provide freedom to be the "fearfully and wonderfully made" individual and writer God means for you to be.

When we discover more about who we are at our core, we don't tout our strengths with pride to anyone who will listen or lord our strengths over others. We also don't excuse negative behaviors as "natural" and "unavoidable."

Personality knowledge is not an excuse for sin. Instead of giving in to a sinful negative trait or even the sin of pride we could have due to a positive trait, we allow God to help us remain humble and dependent on Him. We ask for His guidance in molding our weakness into a God-honoring strength.

In our writing, as in our spiritual lives, this knowledge isn't an excuse for poor choices and habits. Awareness of my traits, both positive and negative, offers me opportunity and caution. Any positive trait, taken to the extreme, becomes a negative. Knowing this, I can be proactive in keeping my actions and attitudes in line with godly ones and those that will help me succeed in my writing goals.

Any negative trait has the potential to be a powerful positive one. Sometimes this is hard to see, but it is true. God can use any trait we have to bless others and to glorify Him.

One of my children has a natural tendency to speak up. As a child, it resulted in talking back and needing the last word. These behaviors often landed him in time out. One day, he wailed that he wished God hadn't given him a mouth.

I encouraged him that if given control, God would use that mouth to speak truth, even in the hard times. The key to turning any negative into a positive is allowing God to control when, where, and how we use it.

As writers, we may not be speaking the truth audibly, but we are speaking truth through our words. And, as with my son, we need to curb our natural tendency to let everything fly and allow God to guide when, where, and how we speak through our keyboards.

Learning who we are does not confine us; it gives us great freedom. This knowledge enables us to appreciate God's design in our lives and see how He might choose to use us. It also gives us the ability to pinpoint weaknesses that our loving Father wants to sweeten into beautiful traits He can use for His glory.

Maybe you've already taken steps to learn about your personality. That's great. I don't care if you found out you're an ABCD, blue with red tendencies, or a buffalo. Many, but not all, personality assessment tools work off the same principles, and once you learn them, it's easy to adjust and find yourself in each one.

As a side note, I do realize there are some systems out there with less than godly origins. Do your research and find one you're comfortable using. I personally know the creators of the LINKED®

Personality System, and I have studied extensively from the system theirs was inspired by. This is a quick and easy way to find out more about God's wonderfully created you. Here's a link to a free online assessment, **https://bit.ly/3zTCN7N**. While the Quick Guide to Personalities book gives more detail, this link is a great place to start finding out about the characteristics that make you a one-of-a-kind specialty blend.

* * *

ACTION STEP

> *Take the personality quiz above or a different one. Write down some of the things you learn about yourself and your approach to tasks, successes, and difficulties.*
>
> *Can you see some of the weaknesses you may struggle to overcome? What about the strengths? How do these characteristics affect your writing life?*

# 2

# GOOD TO THE LAST DROP

Not being a coffee drinker, I'm only moderately successful making a good cup. I start with all the right ingredients. I buy good coffee and fancy-flavored creamers. I mean, what coffee drinker wouldn't enjoy a southern butter pecan coffee? I think it sounds amazing. But, for me, concept and reality are two completely different things.

First, my brew is strong enough to be a champion weightlifter. The next time, it's so weak you'd be just as well off drinking a cup of water. Too much cream. Not enough sugar. The list goes on.

Because I'm unable to taste it, I can't know for certain I've gotten the recipe correct when I make a cup for my husband. Even worse is when I attempt a fancy drink like a flavored, frozen coffee for my sons. Not only is my kitchen a disaster when I finish, but most of the time, I've managed to make only a tolerable drink for my boys.

Procuring the highest-quality ingredients is only the first step. I must know how to blend them together in the best way to produce a drink enjoyable to the last drop. If I refuse to follow a recipe, my hit-or-miss attempt will provide varying results.

Knowing our personality traits is only a first step in learning to write well while doing so in ways that mix perfectly with our God-given design. We must also know what God intends us to make with those ingredients. We need God's recipe to create the perfect cup.

> To be who God wants us to be as writers, we must follow His recipe for our life.

How great would it be if God detailed every part of His plan for us? If somewhere between the Testaments, there was a book with our name on it and verses filling the chapters that pertained directly to us? I'd be ecstatic if Heather Greer 1:1 read, "And God said, let Heather write books to encourage and grow others in their faith."

Talk about a neon sign! That would make things so much easier. So much clearer.

We won't get our own book of the Bible and probably no neon sign. Most of us won't even score a burning bush or talking donkey. And while a positive meeting with an agent or editor can be encouraging, it's not necessarily a sign pointing us down the path of the writer.

Don't let that discourage you. God isn't silent on the recipe for our lives. Many scriptures assure us of God's plans for us and give insight into what our purpose might be. And the big-picture lessons He shares with us are a necessity to incorporate into our writing.

Here are a few of my favorites to consider. Though they are all familiar scriptures, I encourage you not to skip over or skim through them. Take time to meditate on each scripture and ask God what His truth means for your life. Each one, added to our writing, becomes another step in the recipe to creating our perfect writing blend.

> Jeremiah 29:11 NASB—*"For I know the plans that I have for you,' declares the LORD, 'plans for welfare and not for calamity to give you a future and a hope."*

**His truth:** God has plans for us, for our good to give us hope and a future.

> John 15:16 NASB—*"You did not choose Me but I chose you, and appointed you that you would go and bear fruit, and that your fruit would remain, so that whatever you ask of the Father in My name He may give to you."*

**His truth:** We are called to bear God's fruit.

> Philippians 2:1-4 NASB—*"Therefore if there is any encouragement in Christ, if there is any consolation of love, if there is any fellowship of the Spirit, if any affection and compassion, make my joy complete by being of the same mind, maintaining the same love, united in spirit, intent on one purpose. Do nothing from selfishness or empty conceit, but with humility of mind regard one another as more important than yourselves; do not merely look out for your own personal interests, but also for the interests of others."*

**His truth:** We are called to be of one mind in love and humility, looking out for the interests of others, not our own interests only.

> Ephesians 2:10 NASB—*"For we are His workmanship, created in Christ Jesus for good works, which God prepared beforehand so that we would walk in them."*

**His truth:** We are created for good works that God has prepared for us to complete.

> Micah 6:8 NASB—*"He has told you, O man, what is good; And what does the LORD require of you But to do justice, to love kindness, And to walk humbly with your God?"*

**His truth:** We are called to do justice, love mercy, and walk humbly with God, not when it's easy but all the time, in every area of life.

> Romans 12:1-2 NASB—*"Therefore I urge you, brethren, by the mercies of God, to present your bodies a living and holy sacrifice, acceptable to God, which is your spiritual service of worship. And do not be conformed to this world, but be transformed by the renewing of your mind, so that you may prove what the will of God is, that which is good and acceptable and perfect."*

**His truth:** We are called to worship God through offering our entire being, including letting our minds be scrubbed clean of the world's ideas and filled with God's way of thinking and acting.

> 1 Peter 4:10-11 NASB—*"As each one has received a special gift, employ it in serving one another as good stewards of the manifold grace of God. Whoever speaks, is to do so as one who is speaking the utterances of God; whoever serves is to do so as one who is serving by the strength which God supplies; so that in all things God may be glorified through Jesus Christ, to whom belongs the glory and dominion forever and ever. Amen."*

**His truth:** We are called to use our gifts to serve others and bring God glory.

> Ephesians 4:1-3 NASB—*"Therefore I, the prisoner of the Lord, implore you to walk in a manner worthy of the calling with which you have been called, with all humility and gentleness, with patience, showing tolerance for one another in love, being diligent to preserve the unity of the Spirit in the bond of peace."*

**His truth:** We are to live in a way that is worthy of God, being unified with other believers in humility and gentleness.

These scriptures only scratch the surface of who we're called to be and what we're called to do as followers of Christ. Sometimes, we discount these and other scriptures like them because they fail to provide us with the specifics of the unique purpose God has for us to fulfill.

Neglecting these truths would be a mistake. Like our personalities provide a base for understanding how we act and react, these scriptures are the solid foundation each believer must build on to accomplish whatever God tasks us to accomplish in the way He wants us to do it.

No matter what we do, if we do it without a godly attitude, our actions will only end up serving us, not others—and certainly not God. Before seeking our specific area of service, we need to make sure our hearts are in it for the right reasons.

Since you're reading this book, I'm going to assume you feel called to the written word in some way. Whether the dream to write came in your childhood or surprised you as an adult, it has been planted in your heart.

Maybe you're excited about teaching through articles. Your joy may spring from the idea of encouraging others through story. Script writing, blogging, crafting Bible studies, providing children's church take-home papers, writing book reviews. The choices are endless, but they all come down to the dream of writing.

The passion is there. You're learning about the craft of writing through books, conferences, and classes. The local writing group (or virtual one) you're part of provides the support you need for development as a writer. Ideas spring up without any prompting on your part. You've got the right ingredients to create something beautiful. The only thing missing is the recipe to understand how each element blends to craft the finished product.

God is our dream's creator. He gave us our personalities and experiences, our passions, and every other ingredient for the dream. That being the case, shouldn't we seek Him out for how He wants it used and what He considers success for the dream? Shouldn't we confirm that the dream we think we should follow is the dream He means for us?

In *The Dream Giver*, Bruce Wilkinson weaves an allegory much like that of *Pilgrim's Progress*. At one point, the main character gives his dream back to the Dream Giver. Why? Because the Dream Giver gave it in the first place, and the main character needed to know it was the correct dream for his life.

This step is essential. If we don't seek God's plan for the dream, we may be combining all the best ingredients in the wrong amounts. The result isn't a perfectly blended dream. Like my attempts at making coffee, we end up with something tolerable. But who wants tolerable when amazing is available?

The goal isn't for those who partake of our dream to walk away knowing they'll politely decline next time it's offered. Our desire is for others to taste the perfect blend of ingredients coming together in a way that gives God glory and creates desire for more of the same. In this, we fulfill the purposes set out in the scriptures above.

To ensure we're doing what God wants with the ingredients He's given, we offer the dream back to Him. I did this early in my writing. I prayed over the dream, letting God know how much the dream meant to me. I also told Him that being inside His will for my life was my most important goal. If my dream wasn't His dream for me, I didn't want it. And if the desire was from Him but my vision of what it should be was not, I asked Him to correct my sight.

It took time, but God confirmed the dream in my heart in many ways. Now, each time I face periods of discouragement or doubt, I give the dream back to God. Every time, He has confirmed it and returned it to me.

Will that always be the case? I don't know. But I don't have to know if God has another dream waiting. If He does, the new dream will also create something beautiful with the ingredients God provides. Right now, I know the recipe He wants me to use, and I am confident that the results will be good till the last drop.

*You Write You*

\* \* \*

ACTION STEP

*Spend time with the scriptures above. Ask God to show you His plan for the personality, interests, and talents He has given you. Give Him the dream of your heart and listen for His guidance in it.*

# 3

# MIXING IT UP FOR A PERFECT BLEND

Uniquely created and gifted. Tasked with showing others Christ through how we live and what we do. Inspired to follow the dream of writing and encouraged that God has confirmed it in us. We've gathered the correct ingredients. Now, it's time to mix the perfect blend.

But how? How much inspiration is mixed with dedication to create something beautiful that will bring others joy, encouragement, hope, or whatever else God may want to offer through us?

And what do we do with all the recipe notes from other authors who've mixed these same ingredients with great success many times before us? What if the newest writing tool or method they heartily recommend doesn't work for us? Is it a sign that we're chasing the wrong dream?

Let's be real. There are countless methods and tools available to writers today. They aren't limited to the actual process of putting words on the screen. Even down to generating ideas, we find a variety of methods to help. There are tools to organize our research. Programs clean up what we've written prior to submission. With AI, there are even ways to let technology do the work of writing for you, though I am not in favor of any writer using AI for that purpose.

After the words are written, tools and methods exist for organizing the business side of our writing. And there are tried-and-true aids for arranging your writing space and organizing your time to make the best use of both.

Nothing needs to be left to chance. If there's an issue, someone has developed a tool to overcome it. But wait. There's more. With the correct products and methods unleashed in your writing, you, too, can be the next best-selling author!

Sound a little like an infomercial? Maybe a bit too good to be true? Perhaps, it's because methods and products are not one size fits all. And we must consider that as with many of the products sold on television infomercials, reality and the touted benefits do not always line up.

There are times when the product is at fault. Simply put, it doesn't work, for anyone, the way it is supposed to. With today's relative ease of developing and selling products, there are bound to be those that are more like the prize from a Cracker Jack box and less like a toy from FAO Schwarz. They sell you on their quality, but what you receive is far from valuable.

Other times, the issue isn't a semi-fraudulent product. Instead, problems arise when people assume or are led to believe the product will work for every person. Just as our books are not for every reader but a select audience, the products and programs that help authors create them are not for every author.

There are many amazing writing helps on the market. Author friends and conference instructors sing their praises. We invest, eager to experience the wonders of the product. Only, we find it trips us up, slows us down, and frustrates us enough we consider tossing our laptop out the window.

What's wrong with us? Why is everyone else having great success while we can barely muddle through? We've taken the classes to show us how to use it. We've watched the videos and read the instruction books. We know the issue isn't lack of training.

Maybe, it's us. Maybe we're not good enough writers to make it work.

Our failure in finding success can not only cause frustration, but as thoughts like these creep in, they bring discouragement and doubt. As authors, we face enough of these feelings without piling them on because a tool meant for our good isn't working for us. But what can we do?

The good news is we've already started protecting ourselves from unnecessary frustration and doubt. There are three steps in doing so, and we've already covered the first two. Here they are summed up in one place so we can quickly reference them any time there's a need.

**Step One: Pass the Class**

For success with any new product, app, or method, we must possess a teachable spirit. Though often spoken of in relation to our spiritual lives, scripture gives us many examples of and characteristics necessary for a teachable spirit. The principles, though speaking of spiritual things, can be applied to any area of our lives as long as the teachings we consider do not go against the Word of God.

Proverbs 18:15 reminds us that *"The mind of the prudent acquires knowledge, And the ear of the wise seeks knowledge."* To be prudent and wise, we must seek instruction. This requires first having a humble attitude.

We can't learn anything if we can't admit our limitations. Only the perfect need no instruction. I've yet to meet a perfect author. Even focusing on writing alone, we all have areas in need of growth.

There is always an author who has written more prolifically, received greater acclaim, or sold more books. Other authors may be able to craft characters with more depth or, like a master artist, paint the setting with their words in ways we aspire to. When we get stuck in our way of doing things and fail to admit our need, we miss out on valuable skills and attitudes others want to share with us.

In essence, we tell them they have nothing to offer us. This attitude is in direct opposition to the humbleness spoken of in Luke 6:40, which says, *"A pupil is not above his teacher; but everyone, after he has been fully trained, will be like his teacher."*

Before we seek out and test any new product or method, I believe it's important to start with prayer. We can ask God to help us admit when and where we need help. As we consider options, we can ask Him to show us which ones will be best for us. Then, as we begin and frustrations or doubts arise, we can ask Him for patience, understanding, and if needed, someone to physically come alongside us to teach us.

But, we argue, we've been open. We've learned and tried the new, but the results are still lacking. Does this mean this writing aid is not for us to use? Not necessarily.

First, we need to confirm that we have a complete understanding of how the tool is used. Our teachable spirit comes into play beyond simply trying to find the new products or methods to help with our issue. Sometimes it requires seeking out people, either physically or through online tutorials, who know the ins and outs of this new-to-us thing. Writers' conferences are a wonderful place to find these individuals since many of them have workshops tailored to instruction on various methods or products.

Remember we need to be patient with ourselves. There is a learning curve in every new endeavor. Our work won't progress as quickly while we're still adapting to the change. That said, if we've sought instruction with a teachable spirit and have confidence in our understanding of the product, we can determine if we're still in the learning stage or if it's not working for us.

If, after gaining proficiency with the tool, we find ourselves pushing aside the new in favor of the old, we may not be facing a struggle with the learning curve. Our previous methods weren't working, at least on some level. We know that. Returning to what was already broken means the new wasn't working for us either. No matter how many rave reviews it receives, this wonderful tool may not be the new thing that's best for us.

**Step Two: Embrace Your Uniqueness—Not Everything Fits**

We are uniquely created and gifted for God's purpose in our lives. He's given us unique personalities with equally unique blends of strengths and weaknesses.

Knowing this truth helps us keep every detail of our writing lives in perspective. It shapes our content, style, and method.

Let's return for a moment to our earlier coffee talk. My children like iced coffee. My husband does not. His dislike doesn't make iced coffee drinks bad, and it doesn't mean my husband doesn't love coffee. The only thing we can say with 100 percent accuracy is that my husband doesn't love *iced* coffee.

This principle applies to our writing lives as well. A writing aid loved by many but not by me doesn't mean I don't want to be a good writer. The only truth we can claim is I don't like that product. For whatever reason, it doesn't work for me. This shift in perspective frees us from mentally berating ourselves when something fails us. Perhaps, that special thing "everyone else is using" simply wasn't crafted for us.

That brings us to our third and final step in protecting ourselves from discouragement when one size does not fit all. While I've saved it for last in our discussion, it is no less important than the first two steps. As we strive to be the best authors we can be, this step is vital.

**Step Three: Be Like Jesus—Find the Heart**

In the introduction. I shared the depth of discouragement I experienced when every author I sat under for instruction taught about the need to plot. While they may not have meant it as a be all, end all, I never heard any teaching accepting deviation from this method.

- Did I want to prevent holes in my stories? Then, I had to plot.
- Did I want a strong framework, drawing readers in through the end? Then, I had to plot.
- Did I want publishers to take me seriously? Then, I had to plot.
- Did I want a publishing contract? Then, I had to plot.

Let me be clear. Plotting does help create a strong story, free from holes, that publishers take notice of and readers enjoy. But does that mean plotting is the only way to accomplish this? No. It's a tried-and-true method, but it's *one* method. While there are a few things in life with only one way, like salvation coming through Jesus alone, most of the issues we face have more wiggle room built in.

Jesus faced the inflexible during His brief years here on the earth. During His ministry, Jesus spoke with many who were charged with teaching the masses about honoring God through the laws given. Man had, consequently, broken these down into minute tidbits, which were to be adhered to in all circumstances.

These laws were good. How could they not be? They came from God, Himself. Yet, people dissected and analyzed God's original rules. Then, in their desire to avoid any appearance of sin, added their own specific interpretations of how each law should be carried out in the people's day-to-day lives.

These addendums were to be strictly observed. Whether or not they were added sincerely, to honor God through utmost obedience, only He can judge. Regardless of their origin, the caveats created by man forged an environment where those desiring control could micromanage with abandon those in their care.

The people of Jesus's time became slaves to a strict, frustrating, and impossible set of standards. No one argued with these rules, passed down by the powers that be. Until Jesus. When Jesus's public ministry began, the status quo was rocked.

Luke 6 emphasizes this problem. Take a moment to read this familiar passage. Don't skim over it. Instead, read it prayerfully, asking God to show what we can glean for use in the writing ministries He's blessed us with.

> *"On another Sabbath He entered the synagogue and was teaching; and there was a man there whose right hand was withered. The scribes and the Pharisees were watching Him closely to see if He healed on the Sabbath, so that they might find reason to accuse Him. But He knew what they were thinking, and He said to the man with the withered hand, 'Get up and come forward!' And he got up and came forward. And Jesus said to them, 'I ask you, is it lawful to do good or to do harm on the Sabbath, to save a life or to destroy it?' After looking around at them all, He said to him, 'Stretch out your hand!' And he did so, and his hand was restored."*
> (Luke 6:6-11)

Jesus understood the laws and how the Pharisees would use them against Him. He also knew the Pharisees missed something important in their zealousness. In their efforts to find infractions, they overlooked or ignored the purpose of the laws they enforced. In attempts to prove their righteousness and the unrighteousness of others, they ignored the needs of the people and the reasons God gave the laws in the first place.

In the Sermon on the Mount recorded in the book of Matthew, Jesus makes clear His stance on the law. Where the passage we read in Luke highlighted the Pharisees' tendencies to overlook love in favor of law, this passage from Matthew warns against using God's rules as rigid markers of the minimum required for lawfulness. To Jesus, murder and hate are two sides of the same coin. He taught that generosity isn't stopping with what's required but giving from the heart.

His teachings echo God's declarations in the Old Testament regarding sacrifices. God finds no pleasure in sacrificing for sacrifice's sake. His purpose in creating the sacrificial system wasn't to obligate people or give them reason for pride in their piousness. The systems God put in place were for the good of the people, to show their need for Him and point them to His provision. God wanted obedience from His people, but He desired, and still desires, for obedience to come from a place of love for Him.

Doing the right things for the wrong reasons. God's people struggled with this in the Old Testament, and the tendency was still prevalent in Jesus's time on earth. The people missed a key element in their worship, sacrifice, and rule-following. They missed the heart behind their actions.

This spiritual truth is as relevant for us as it was for God's people in the Bible. It's also a principle we can use in our writing ministries. While nothing man creates is good in the same way God's laws are good, and they fall miserably short of His perfection, we have many helps available to us as writers.

Task tracking calendars, character development sheets, writing programs that track every element of our projects, and social media apps that post at scheduled times are all beneficial in a writer's life. They can be immensely helpful in creating productive workspaces, strong stories, and effective marketing strategies.

 *Each writing aid has a heart, a purpose. Find it.*

However, when we put our time and resources into learning and implementing these things and find they aren't working, we don't have to throw our hands up in frustration. Giving up is not our only option. It's not even our best option. We have a recourse.

Unlike God's laws, which were perfectly made for everyone, all the time, man-made author helps are not universal. While they work well for some, they may fail for others. Whether or not each one offers success for us, we need to remember they were made with specific goals in mind.

The answer for us, as Jesus pointed out in dealing with the Pharisees, is returning to the heart. The Pharisees missed God's purpose for His laws, choosing instead doing for doing's sake. Writers need to avoid the same trap.

Using the many writing aids available to us is wonderful, but they are meant to help us. When they don't, we need to examine why.

In questioning the why, we may find the reason the program failed us. Or we may find we failed the program. Determining whether the failure belongs to the program or to us is only the beginning. Before we toss the tool aside completely, we should examine the heart of each author help and determine what the tool is meant to strengthen in us.

When we know the issue being corrected or helped, we can find alternatives to accomplish the same thing. With the abundance of products and programs on the market, finding one that complements our God-given personality and writing style is almost a certainty.

This is not to say finding the right tools will foster a forever frustration-free writing environment. Many writing irritations have nothing to do with the author helps we use. However, the overall process becomes less frustrating and doubt-inducing when we match the writing issue and our personality with writing aids that fit the needs of both.

As we continue, we're going to focus on some of the more popular areas of the writing life where authors get bogged down in frustration. We'll get to the heart, the why, of each aid and lay out alternatives to meet each need. Though I hope we find successful ones for each of us, no list I can present will be exhaustive.

The market is growing every day. This is another area where knowing the heart behind the aid comes in handy. If the offerings inside these pages don't fit, we're still one step closer to finding what will. As we discover each writing aid's purpose, that knowledge helps us find a tool we can be successful with that fulfills the same goal.

While the internet has made searching for alternatives quick and easy in some respects, we do need to do our due diligence. Not every product is created equal. Do your research. There are writing aids that promise the stars, but the products leave you stranded on earth.

Don't take a website's word about the veracity of their product. Check out reviews, especially independent reviews. Look at positive and negatives as this will give the clearest picture of where the product excels and falls short. Ask about the product in author groups. When available, take a class on the writing aid at a conference. Use free trials and tutorials when offered.

We must remember, the best writing aid will not only help us with the issue but also be one we will use.

\* \* \*

ACTION STEP

> *Consider some of the writing tools or methods you've tried but failed in using. Ask God to show you if your heart was teachable when you tried to apply this writing help. Did you give yourself enough opportunity to learn how to use this tool effectively? For those writing aids that didn't work after trying to learn them with the right attitude and ample time, reflect on what element of each one didn't work for you and why. Keep this list handy as we go into the next section of the book.*

# 4

# YOUR WRITING WORLD

As we begin the practical discussion of writing methods and programs, there is an abundance of possible starting points. Understanding how our creative process works is a vital discussion for this book. The outflow of our creativity—seeing our characters spring to life and our plots lived out on the page—is the fulfilling part of our writing journeys.

But the *how* of creating isn't the only element worthy of our focus.

Sitting in our chairs, typing furiously, and watching the story unfold feel like the starting point. They're not. There are additional facets to our writing that demand our attention. Environmental factors have a large influence over our productivity.

Our physical setting, the one we're working in—not the one we're creating—is important. Even considering a basic element such as this, writing experts have added their beliefs about how a successful writer's world will look. Focusing on our writing space may not seem pivotal, but it can put us at ease in our writing, allowing creativity to flow with fewer hindrances.

- Have a dedicated place for writing.
- Make this place a distraction-free zone. No dirty dishes, loads of laundry, or stack of bills in your line of sight.
- Set your phone to silent.
- Have everything you need in one place, from reference materials to your laptop and your writing snack of choice.

On the surface, these seem like simple mandates. They make perfect sense on paper, but books aren't written on paper. Okay. Yes, they are. But writers don't always peacefully co-exist with plans on paper as they're writing those books because life happens.

Writers are everywhere, in every stage of life. High school graduates eagerly seek the realization of their authoring dreams. Budding young adult writers, balancing the needs of family and working full-time to pay the bills, hold fast to their God-given dream of publication. Empty-nesters with distraction-free evenings and retirees who make writing their full-time focus, write with passion, God-given talents, and a lifetime of experiences.

As faith-based writers, we're united by a common goal, no matter our stage of life. Everything we create is done to honor God with the talent and passion He's given. Whether we write strictly faith-filled books or produce clean fiction from a biblical worldview, we share His truth with the world through our words. Though this thread ties us together, life's demands forge a variety of paths to accomplish our tasks.

My writing journey has not been one of sole focus. The path I walked wasn't the Hollywood version of writing. I didn't have the funds to jet off to the far corners of the world to write in distraction-free bliss. There was no month in a mountain cabin with nature's inspiration as my only writing companion.

My writing dreams began in my elementary school library. They solidified with my first creative writing assignment in fourth grade. I loved stories, and it was exciting to learn I didn't have to limit myself to reading them. I could tell the stories myself.

In high school, my dream became muddled. During my senior year, I met the man I would marry. Writing seemed impractical, maybe even irresponsible, as I considered a future with a family that would need regular income.

I entered college expecting a creative writing or teaching degree. And though I took advantage of many classes in both studies, I never attained that degree. After my children were born, I stopped classes to care for them. While I've never regretted that choice, it ended my time in college. Instead of English-teacher-by-day and writer-by-night, going back to work meant accepting less-fulfilling jobs to pay the bills.

My dream took the back burner until the Holy Spirit whispered to return to what I was passionate about. By this stage of life, I'd long since passed the carefree high school and college days. Instead of freedom of time and money, I worked full-time as a receptionist. Three of my four children were not yet in their teens. And I was a pastor's wife, active in various ministries in the church. Demands of others ordered my twenty-four-hour days. My house was full of people and the noise and activity they created.

With four children and a limited budget, we couldn't afford an office. Even if we could, every space in the house was occupied. And those spaces were far from conducive for concentration.

My bedroom was my only escape. Far from an ideal solution and one I had to wait to enjoy each night.

First, there was supper to cook and homework to complete. Then, if my husband was home from working his multiple jobs, I could flee to my room with my laptop. A television tray held my laptop. The bed served as my chair.

Even sequestered in my room, concentration was not a given. Four active children create noise. I've never been able to block out senseless noise. To this day, if the television is on or my husband is doom-scrolling videos on his phone, I can't focus.

My solution to the cacophony? Headphones. Though I naturally craved silence, I adapted to writing with earbuds in and music playing. My brain could make sense of the song and filter out the extraneous and disjointed noise of boys wrestling and holding Nerf wars in the house.

Even in this time, I was blessed. I have friends who write at the kitchen table, surrounded by the debris of school projects and dirty dishes. They do this while their children move freely about them in play or disagreement with siblings or whatever each day may bring. They adapt as best they can.

Currently, I'm an empty-nester. I now enjoy a space dedicated to writing and my creative process. Instead of seeing only piles of laundry, toys, and dishes, I can now look out at the peaceful view of our backyard and gain inspiration.

At this stage, I am my biggest hurdle to distraction-free and focus-filled writing. I scroll social media too often. I answer the phone when it rings. When I take a break, I seem to forget it's only temporary and allow what's outside the office to steal my attention.

I share my situation for two reasons.

The first is as encouragement. Wherever you are in following the path to your writing dreams, your situation will change. Little ones won't be underfoot forever. There is an end to homework and evening events at the school. While there will always be laundry and dishes, there will, eventually, be less of them.

*Wherever you are in following the path to your writing dreams, your situation will change.*

Enjoy your children and the chaos they bring. The end of those things will come too soon. They are one of your most important life priorities, second only to God and spouse.

Don't resent those precious distractions. Their presence doesn't take away your hope for writing. Not even when you can't create the quiet, distraction-free environment many experts tell you is needed.

When expectation and reality don't match, disappointment and frustration can set in. Externally imposed expectations still usher in these feelings, maybe even more than personal expectations. We can convince ourselves to adjust our ideas of what life as a writer should look like. But when one of the experts paints a clear picture of what it takes to be a writer, their ideas are a little harder to ignore.

The rules regarding how your writing space should look become an impossible weight. There is no place for a dedicated space in your home. Noise and activity abound. Escaping the distractions is a wonderfully unattainable fantasy.

Frustration and discouragement may be your companions right now, but there is a way to send them packing. A look at the *why* of these instructions offers a perspective shift to free you from the load you carry.

Freedom through understanding the purpose of the rule is my second reason for sharing my experience.

- We're told to dedicate a space tailored to our writing. Why?
- We're told to keep it free of clutter and chores and ringing phones. Why?
- Why do we need to gather everything we could possibly need in the one place we've chosen to write?

Two words: Distraction and productivity.

Ditching distractions allows focus. Singular focus increases productivity. Consistent production equals more written or edited or marketed pages produced in a timely manner. When we rid ourselves of distractions, we can give ourselves to the work of writing and accomplish our goals.

Production is at the heart of pushing for a dedicated space. But for some, it feels like an impenetrable wall blocking our success. Whether we live in a tiny apartment or have children taking up every inch of living space, specifying an area for our creative pursuit is impossible. Our families demand our time, and their noise reverberates through every nook and cranny of our homes.

But, as I said, there is hope. The siren song of writing doesn't have to wait until a new life stage arrives. Our dedicated space may look different from those of other writers. It's okay. The goal, the reason for a designated spot, is lessened distractions and increased productivity. With a little ingenuity, we can accomplish this.

I'm not a morning person, but I know many who are. If you're an early bird, freedom from distractions may be rising before the rest of the family wakes. When your time and energy aren't required by everyone else, even a lap desk in the corner recliner can become a dedicated space.

Likewise, night owls can find their space of solitude after everyone else has gone to sleep. With the day successfully ended for the family, the stories filling your mind through the daylight hours can become your focus. Whether at the kitchen table or sitting on the couch, your dedicated space can grow your productivity.

The solution may not be as simple as changing your sleep habits. I'm neither a morning person nor a night owl. According to the rest-tracking app on my phone, I have a mid-morning and early afternoon spike in my ability to be productive. I get one additional burst later in the evening, according to the app, but I haven't found that one yet. I've always been this way.

In my early writing days, these productive hours were sucked dry by my nine-to-five job. Many face the same situation. Even for us, there is hope.

Finding a sweet spot for writing may not be as easy, but it is possible. First, don't beat yourself up for the less-than-stellar writing you accomplish during the weekdays when you squeeze in time between dinner and bedtime. Give yourself grace. Then, take advantage of those precious times when you're able to work during your most productive hours. Use them to polish what you previously wrote. Soon, your work will shine, and no one will be the wiser.

Your productive space and times may require fluidity. What works one day, may not the next. Family needs are ever-shifting, and for a time, our writing space may need flexibility too.

Whether your space is static or in flux, the experts agree—we need to make our area conducive to work. I've listened to those who promote an almost spartan or sterile environment. No distractions. No laundry in our line of sight. No dishes beckoning from the sink. And no extraneous decorations to arrest our attention, if we're blessed with an office.

All work, no play. Keep your mind on the task at hand. No phones, and absolutely no non-writing-related internet searches. In fact, don't do *any* internet searches. Make a note in your manuscript, keep writing, and look it up later.

While a case exists for considering the heart over the letter of mandates on our physical writing environment, one rule stands apart as one we should follow to the best of our ability. Unlike other environmental writing rules, this one doesn't deal with aesthetics or increasing productivity. It's about you retaining your physical ability to write and live well.

Keep your writing space as ergonomically correct as possible.

Ensuring your body stays in the least-damaging position possible while you're writing is key to continuing your writing without pain as you age. Taking steps to position your body correctly can also help you avoid future surgeries from Repetitive Strain Injuries (RSI). Writing is a sedentary pursuit that not only keeps us still, it also keeps us in one position longer than is healthy.

We need to be proactive in protecting our bodies while we write. A healthy body will keep us writing, free from the aggravating and even debilitating distractions of painful joints and muscles.

Apart from keeping our area as ergonomic as possible, there is leeway when we consider productivity and our writing space. Our area doesn't need to be functional for every writer. We tailor our writing space only to ourselves. Our desk may be a lap desk or a small moveable desk. Some, like me when I started, may have only a television tray. Whatever works for you, set up as ergonomically correct as possible, will make your space conducive to writing.

Laptop on and work in progress open, you settle in for a

productive writing time. At first, you do wonderfully. The words flow. Before long, sentences turn into paragraphs, which turn into pages. Then, it happens. Distraction.

Maybe you look up from your screen as you struggle to find the right word. A noise may have pulled your attention away. Whatever the reason, you look away from the screen and find dust bunnies on the floor, clean clothes overflowing their basket, or dishes piled high next to the sink.

Seeing them makes them real. Acknowledging them gives them space in your mind. Suddenly, they're all you can think about. But, no. You're writing. You don't have time to take care of those pesky clothes. You focus on the screen once more, but as your mind struggles for the perfect word, the only thing you can focus on is the mess you're trying so hard to ignore.

Finally, you give up. Completing the task will take only a few minutes. Then, you can write in peace. Only as you're completing the first, another inevitably takes its place. A few more minutes won't hurt. So, you begin the second task. Then, a third. Before long, you've eaten up your entire block of writing time without writing at all.

Maybe tomorrow will be better.

It doesn't have to be like this. There are ways to combat those pesky chores trying to pull you away from your writing. At times when my office is unusable, I write in a room with open visibility to the kitchen. Dishes tend to litter the sink and counters. When the words aren't flowing, it's easy for me to fall prey to the siren song of the chore. After all, dishes need cleaning. I'm being productive in a different way.

Only this productivity never leads to words on a page. At least, it doesn't for me. Dishes do not inspire me. Ever.

One way I've learned to combat this distraction is through a change in my routine. Dishes washed in the morning never leave my sink empty. There is always someone adding to it. However, if I wash every dish right before bed, the next morning, during my prime writing time, the sink and counters remain empty and distraction-free.

The odd dish or two left in the sink after breakfast usually hide from my sight, allowing me to ignore them. But when I take a movement break from my computer, I wash these too. This allows me to be productive in my home without sacrificing writing time.

Whenever a chore or distraction tempts you from the keyboard, I encourage you to experiment with ways to complete those tasks right before your most productive writing times. When you can't complete them, can you disguise or hide them? Out of sight, out of mind.

With or without an office, noise is an issue at times. For some, silence prevents productivity. The lack of sound is distracting. These writers thrive surrounded by noise and activity.

For others, every little sound pulls them away from their work. Or they find that some sounds are easy to block out while others break their concentration every time.

We're unique. You may even find yourself somewhere in the middle of these extremes. The key is knowing how God wired you as a person and working within those parameters.

The long months of the Covid lockdown were difficult for me in ways I never expected. Initially, I loved staying home and having a reason to tell people I couldn't commit to things. Being home also provided me with extra writing time. As wonderful an opportunity as this was, one small change crumbled my new writing paradise. My husband joined the ranks of those working from home. Our offices shared a wall.

My husband connects with people. It's 90 percent of his job. This meant Zoom meetings and phone calls for eight hours every day. When he took breaks, he watched videos on his phone, started laundry, or banged around in the kitchen.

God gifted me with a husband who is my opposite. We often balance each other out. However, during those long months at home, together 24/7, those differences became hinderances. My husband could ignore my noise to complete his work. I did not have that particular superpower.

Every phone call, meeting, or garbled video pulled me away from what I was writing. Frustration rose. I was on a deadline, and yet, I couldn't ask him not to do his job.

If you find yourself in a noisy situation beyond your control, don't give in to the frustration. Instead, try finding alternate ways to deal with the noise. This may mean investing in a good pair of noise-canceling headphones.

For me, it meant putting in my earbuds and listening to music. While my children were still rambunctious at home, I learned to write to music to tune out their chaos. As I continued writing, I even wrote to music with words. Not only did writing to music help direct my mood toward the tone I wanted to create, but the music also helped me tune out the chaotic noise my mind inevitably focused on while I was attempting to write.

Writing with music is not for everyone. Many people find themselves distracted by the lyrics or changes in rhythm or volume of a song. They can tune out the senseless noise that drives me crazy but can't ignore a song they love.

Maybe headphones and music don't provide the answer for you. Can you find a library, park, or another quiet place to write? For you, the hassle of relocating may be worth it for the words you'll put on the page. I've even known some writers who rent space where they can write in peace.

Those with a dedicated writing space may contend with issues beyond noise and chores. Some authors advocate for writing areas free of anything beyond items specific to writing. Others find those limitations sterile and at odds with their creativity.

Pictures and knickknacks around the room add a personal touch, but they can also be a distraction for some. To rid their space of timewasters, these writers may need to create a more traditional office environment to avoid minute-wasting trips down memory lane.

For others, these personal items are a source of inspiration. They're reminders of important people and events in our lives, the reason we do what we do. They spark imagination and creativity.

I have a painting of a tree by a lake. The landscape is full of rich colors, almost fantastical. While parts of the image remind me of summer, others are very much fall.

Looking at that painting, I picture myself in that world. The life and beauty of the image put me in a creative space. Though it inspires me, the abundant use of color might be distracting for others. They may prefer a simple quote or nothing at all. Use whatever inspires you and create a haven of creativity, no matter what others may say your space should look or feel like.

To lessen other distractions, regular play breaks can be scheduled. At the designated time, scroll through social media, play a game, or call a friend—without guilt. Rather than using a set time for these activities, some might find making those activities a reward for completing a set of tasks works best.

If we lack self-discipline, we may need to set a timer to remind us to continue working, or we may need to forgo those types of breaks until the work is done. Instead, we could choose to take a ten-minute walk. Not only are walks good for our physical health, but they can also boost our creativity.

Designating a space for our writing is possible. We're writers. Creativity is what we do. Let's apply that to the problem and find solutions that work for us. Honoring the heart of finding a dedicated space doesn't require an office completely free of noise and demands. If we can decrease the distraction to increase our productivity, we've honored the heart of the instruction.

ACTION STEP

*What are your biggest obstacles in securing a dedicated space?*

*Write these down. Ask God to show you how you can best solve these issues while remaining faithful to the needs of your family. Walk through each room of your house. Which ones have the best potential for ditching distractions? Remember, it may not be a functional writing space yet. You're looking for potential. Don't settle. Find the one that will best fit your needs.*

*Organization of the space can come after you choose it. What else might you need to fight distraction? Don't forget to incorporate these into your writing space.*

# 5

# NO TIME LIKE THE PRESENT

Real writers write every day. For many of us, this mantra is held up as the standard to measure ourselves by. If we're not writing every day, can we call ourselves writers? No. Not according to the well-intentioned instruction we receive.

We're given a pass if we manage to write any number of words. Even fifty new words on the page elevates us to the rank of real writer. Those meager words can be complete garbage. It doesn't matter. Writers write, and we've written. And we must do it every day.

Depending on who you're listening to, there is some variation in this edict. Instead of a word count, we may instead focus on uninterrupted writing for a set amount of time. But whether we count success in words or minutes, if we fail to write, we fail to be writers.

There is one issue with this rigid way of defining what it means to be a writer.

Life happens.

Illness, either our own or a loved one's, derails our ability to write. Work, church, family obligations, schoolwork, our kids' extracurricular activities, and tidying our homes can all stuff our schedules as full as a Thanksgiving turkey. There are times when the demands placed on us leave no extra hours in the twenty-four we've all been given.

Completing each task on our to-do list can leave us fatigued. Sleep and rest are also necessities for good mental, physical, and emotional health. Besides, we can barely keep our eyes open, much less focus our brains long enough to write. Coherency in what we write? That's a fairy tale when exhaustion hits.

One day, we fail to fulfill the write every day command. A tiny seed of regret pushes through, but we had a great reason. We can ignore it. More than one day without following this rule, and we find ourselves with a fully grown guilt weed.

The words of those master writers come back to haunt and taunt us. Those who don't write, aren't writers. Maybe we're no longer a writer? Is there a sliding scale somewhere that can show us how far off the mark we've wandered?

I fully agree with the truth in the statement that writers must write. I may have worked in a doctor's office once, but that didn't make me a doctor or even a nurse. My scrubs didn't transform me from receptionist to medical professional. Being a doctor or nurse required the schooling of those professions and then doing the work that accompanied the job description. I answered phones and scheduled appointments. I didn't examine or diagnose.

What was true for me in the doctor's office is true in every profession. To be given a label, to be considered one who does a particular thing, we must do that thing. Writing is not an exception.

However, when we take an all-or-nothing approach to our writing, guilt and doubt are our only rewards. Neglecting the heart of this principle leaves us questioning whether God truly confirmed our dream when we gave it back to Him.

While periodically inquiring of God regarding our dreams ensures we're following His path and doing it His way, living in a place of constant frustration and question keeps us from moving at all. Instead, we must cling to the heart of *writers must write every day*.

Why do the masters proclaim this rule from nearly every conference stage? Regular writing enhances our ability to write well and increases our productivity. But the benefits of writing every day are about more than simply being better at what we do. Daily writing also shows commitment to what we say we desire. Commitment, as seen through our actions, elevates us from *dreaming* of being a writer to *being* a writer.

Keeping this purpose in mind, the question becomes, can we fail to write a least a few sentences every day and still be committed to writing? Yes, it is possible. However, it opens us up to a thought process we need to be wary of, and it begins with a follow-up question.

How many days can we miss and still be committed? In working with youth, I've seen the same pattern of thinking when talking about abstinence. They'll admit that sex before marriage is wrong, and, in the next breath, ask, "How far is too far?"

My answer to both writers and teens is the same: You're asking the wrong question.

When we engage in this way of thinking, we're entering a rigid rules-based arena. Our focus becomes what I can get away with and still consider myself in the right. Boundaries and staying inside them become our goal instead of honoring God with the dream He entrusted to us.

Many stories in scripture, both from the Old and New Testaments, highlight the misuse of God's gifts. Samson didn't treasure his gift and allowed worldly pursuits to distract him from his calling, with disastrous results. Solomon, with all the wisdom God gifted him, chose to ignore Godly wisdom and took wives who didn't share his faith. Again, the results were devastating—not only to him but to an entire nation.

The New Testament gives us parables from the prodigal who squandered his gifts on selfish pursuits to the servant who buried the money his master gave him out of fear. In both, we see truth play out again and again. God's gifts are meant to be used for His glory.

Scripture is also clear that activity for activity's sake is not a worthy pursuit. God takes pleasure not in our output but in our attitude. Psalm 51:16-17 reminds us, *"For You do not delight in sacrifice, otherwise I would give it; You are not pleased with burnt offering. The sacrifices of God are a broken spirit; A broken and contrite heart, O God, You will not despise."*

This is just one of several Old Testament scriptures God uses to remind us that the physical acts of sacrifice God instituted in the books of the Law were not what pleased Him. Instead, God's pleasure and displeasure came from understanding the spirit with which sacrifices were offered.

We may be tempted to dismiss this teaching because it's from the old covenant. We no longer sacrifice, so this scripture has no bearing on our lives. Instead of deeming it unprofitable or unapplicable, we can look to the New Testament for further teachings that reinforce the spirit of the verse for our lives.

Jesus called the Pharisees white-washed sepulchers because their actions looked right, but inside, their spirits were dead. 2 Corinthians 9:7 cautions us that *"Each one must do just as he has purposed in his heart, not grudgingly or under compulsion, for God loves a cheerful giver."*

In Colossians chapter three, Paul speaks about being one body, letting God's word dwell in us, teaching, and worshiping with thankfulness. He instructs us to keep the body of Christ and our own spiritual lives healthy. In verse seventeen, he goes further with this admonition: *"Whatever you do in word or deed, do all in the name of the Lord Jesus, giving thanks through Him to God the Father."*

A little farther down, in verses twenty-three and twenty-four, when speaking more about our earthly roles than our roles in the body of Christ, we find the phrasing, *"Whatever you do, do your work heartily, as for the Lord rather than for men, knowing that from the Lord you will receive the reward of the inheritance. It is the Lord Christ whom you serve."*

From beginning to end, the difference is found in the attitude of the heart. It isn't about having perfect attendance at our writer's desk or meeting every goal we set for ourselves. The truth of our commitment is found in our attitudes.

*From beginning to end, the difference is found in the attitude of the heart.*

We've all heard and probably repeated the phrase, "You make time for what you really want." While this is fundamentally true, it doesn't tell the complete story. There are times when our life choices create a barrier between what we want and what we must do.

To honor God in every area of our lives, including our writing, our priorities must be in line with God's priorities. There are times when, after working our nine-to-five job, we come home to children who need additional help with school projects. Caring for a sick loved one or even dealing with our own illness can zap our ability to concentrate and our energy to work. Sometimes, we're faced with setting aside our writing to help a struggling friend deal with difficult life experiences.

Whatever the situation, it demands the scant time and energy we've reserved for writing. Our lofty aspirations to write every day are set aside. But the burden of guilt can be lifted off our shoulders when we grasp that, for a time, and sometimes for a season, we can set our writing aside without stripping away the dream forever.

It's all about the attitude.

Before moving on from the idea that writers must write every day, I want to offer a word of caution. Sometimes, we simply choose to give priority to other activities. It's tempting to say, "Heather told me I don't have to write every day to be a writer. So, I'm good."

Again, we turn to scripture for a spiritual principle we can harness for our writing purposes. In Romans, Paul addresses believers' beliefs that because they have grace, they shouldn't be concerned about their continued sins. Using very forceful language, he corrects them. Sinning to experience more grace or sinning without care because grace is available is an absolute no.

Failure to write every day is not a sin, even for those who feel God has called them to write. However, when we apply the type of thinking present in this verse to our writing, we get back to the heart of the write every day rule and can keep ourselves in check.

Just as we don't continue sinning because we have grace, we don't put off writing just because we can. Complete honesty with ourselves is a necessity when considering this principle and every other principle within these pages.

- Are we making excuses to avoid doing what God called us to do?
- Are we putting other things, avoidable things, before what God is asking of us?
- Are we approaching our writing as if we're doing it for God?

If our answer to the first two questions is yes or our answer to the third one is a no, then we're at serious risk of falling outside the heart of the write-every-day rule. We lie to ourselves when we try to claim it as truth. While we can continue deceiving ourselves for a time, we can't fool God. He knows our hearts.

It all comes down to our attitude.

* * *

ACTION STEP

If you're struggling with guilt or doubt because you've been unable to write every day, I encourage you to pray for God to show you the attitude of your heart. Are you truly committed and giving your all for God's call? If not, ask God to show you where you need to adjust your days to create the time to do what He's called you to do. If this is one of those times you need to extend yourself grace to fail, seek His wisdom in picking up your pen again. If you're not struggling with finding the time to write, there's still a reason to seek God in your writing. Ask Him to show you where your attitude has slipped from one of cheerful giver to going through the motions of sacrifice without an invested heart.

# 6

## TAKING RESPONSIBILITY

Before tackling another writing rule, we need to talk about practical help for those who've searched their hearts and found they're using grace as an excuse to neglect self-discipline in writing.

Growing up in the '80s, there was a phrase associated with a popular cartoon. Whether you watched G.I. Joe or not, you heard and most likely used the phrase, "Knowing is half the battle." I never thought about it as a kid, but if knowing a problem is only half the battle, then what's the other half? You can't win a fight stopping halfway through it.

Knowing comes first. After accepting the problem, taking responsibility for the lesson we've learned is the next step. Without putting action behind our knowledge, we can never overcome the issue we face.

Recently, I've found the work I do as a virtual assistant, an assistant producer on two podcasts, and a church secretary have interfered with my productivity. That's not even counting the interruptions and demands of my family, my home, and our pets. I knocked my word count out of the park when at writing retreats, but on my own, my numbers dwindled. My time at the keyboard was spent with other work. Days went by. Then weeks. Then a month. No new words appeared on any of my works in progress.

- Did my other work need to be completed? Yes.
- Did I find it too easy to neglect writing after a full day of those other pursuits? Yes.
- Did I have the self-discipline to make myself write each week? No, I did not.

My answer may surprise you. After all, this is a book of encouragement for writers, and I just admitted I went months without writing a word. I'm asking you to be honest with yourselves in this process. I believe you should know I demand no less of myself.

Did I want to write? Not enough to prompt me to sit at the keyboard.

The best I could say is that I wanted *the want* to write. I wanted to honor this ministry God has blessed me with, but I fell horribly short. I'm a low-energy, low-attention-span kind of girl. Changing hats multiple times a day wore me out.

This was one of those times grace became an excuse. I wasn't keeping true to the heart of the write every day rule. Developing better time management wasn't even a thought. I deceived myself and received false comfort from the idea that I didn't have to be so legalistic with my writing.

Above all else, I want to stand before God and know I've done all He has asked me to do. Writing is one of those things, at least for this season. Yet, each day yielded the same results. I needed help.

*Above all else, I want to stand before God and know I've done all He asks me to do.*

I needed accountability.

People balk at this word. If the idea is positive, what stops them from seeking accountability in their writing? They know they'll fail. With failure, especially failure in front of others, comes guilt. If you're in this place, I encourage you to check your attitudes and motives.

Why would you feel guilt about not reaching the goal? Would it be because you felt someone else was judging you? Or is it because you knew in yourself your priorities were mixed, and you aren't ready to face it yet?

For me, accountability isn't about a word count. It's not about meeting a writing goal or deadline, though both of those are valid ways to set up your accountability group. Mine isn't even about a group. One of my accountability groups contains two people, the other three—including me in each.

In speaking with another writer in my local writing group, I realized we were both allowing other things to pull us away from writing. I saw it in her before I recognized it in myself. I know. I know. Take out your plank before you point out their splinter.

I'm thankful I didn't try removing her splinter before God spoke clearly to me. I felt it in my spirit. There was no question where the words originated. *You're doing the same thing.*

No, I'm not. I've published several books. Obviously, I am giving myself to my writing.

*How long has it been since you wrote?*

It's a little slump. Nothing to worry about.

*How long?*

I was surprised to learn that a full month had gone by with no new words to show for it. Wow. Had I really gone that long? When did I stop missing the pouring out of a story and itch to get back to it?

*Pot meet kettle.*

God was right. We both needed a partner in self-discipline. Strictly speaking, I guess if another is involved, it's not truly self-discipline, just discipline. Whatever word you choose, it means sitting our rears in chairs, working on whatever project we need to finish.

"What if we agree to two hours writing together every week?" My friend offered the option. "We'll go to the library where nothing else can interfere, and we'll just write."

No lofty word count goals to meet. No looming deadlines crushing us with their weight. Just two hours a week dedicated to nothing but writing. The only way to feel the sting of guilt would be not showing up. Judgment and guilt-free writing accountability? That was my kind of accountability group. I agreed.

Other than the occasional college students talking too loudly for a library—(What happened to old lady librarians shushing people? We need to reinstitute that.)—the only sound for those two hours was the clack of fingers on keys or the music playing through my earbuds (if those people wouldn't be quiet). Marla and I might exchange a few words when we met, when we were walking out, or if one of us was stuck on something. Other than that, we typed.

It's amazing what can be accomplished in two hours.

If the idea of deadlines and word count goals causes you anxiety or dread, consider this type of accountability group. It's low pressure. All you need to do is show up and write.

Even those without local writing friends can find a way to make it work. Do you have a friend with a quiet hobby like crochet, embroidery, sketching, or scrapbooking? Something portable? Consider meeting with them. While they do their thing, you can do yours.

It may also work to have a long-distance partner. Do you have a writing friend you can get online with once a week? Log in, say hi, and spend the next two hours in silence as you write together, apart.

What about those who thrive on the challenge of goals and deadlines? Go ahead and form a more traditional accountability group. Without the writing time aspect, this style works well even virtually. When choosing this method of accountability, take care to avoid guilting or judging those who don't make their goals. Grace and truth can co-exist and do wonders for keeping relationships intact.

There are no rules on how an accountability group should be set up. Recently, two writer friends I met at a conference and I formed an accountability group. Each of us was a bit hesitant about joining a group, so we took time to define what our calls should look like and our expectations of our meetings.

All three of us wanted a successful group that encouraged us to stay on track. And we wanted to avoid guilt. We agreed to no finger-wagging if one of us failed. Instead, we'd encourage each other to begin again. And, if one of us failed consistently, we encouraged that one to reevaluate their goals.

Our group meets virtually once a month, and we have each other's phone numbers for emergency texts for encouragement or prayer. We each set a couple of small goals, and we check on our progress during each call. We pray for each other and celebrate each other's victories, even the small ones.

Your group could operate the same way. Or you may want to add a brainstorming element to the group. Or possibly have the same goal for every person, if all agree. You could have a small group or a large one. And while it is ideal to have an accountability group with other writers who understand what you're struggling with, if there are no other writers available to meet with you in-person or virtually, look for someone else who needs accountability.

They may need encouragement to exercise or eat right while your focus is on writing, but you both need the encouragement of someone who will pray for you, support you when you fail, and celebrate your successes.

* * *

ACTION STEP

Start with prayer. Ask God to show you if an accountability group is right for you and to lead you to those who would make great partners. If you have an initial negative reaction to the mention of accountability, ask God to show you the reason behind your hesitation. When you're ready, one place to look for accountability partners is through your local writing group or writers you connect with at writing conferences.

Before you begin seeking others to join you, take the time to write out what you're looking for specifically. This can help you articulate the group's purpose and alleviate the fears of those you speak with about partnering with you.

# 7
# CHRISTIAN WRITERS WRITE CHRISTIAN CONTENT

"I get so discouraged."

If you've been writing long, you've probably heard this sentiment. It flows from the mouth of the published and unpublished alike. The explanation following the phrase is different from person to person. On this occasion, my friend's attitude came from feeling pressured to write Christian fiction simply because she is a Christian.

Many writers of faith struggle with the same feelings of doubt and disillusionment. Their writing is clean and even uplifting but not expressly faith-based. This battle is easily seen in the variety of speculative sub-genres.

When you're an author dealing with fantasy worlds, direct correlation of their gods to our God can be a bit difficult. In dystopian societies where government has assumed tight control, there may be no religion left. Some Christian authors choose to write allegorically. The faith we know is evident, the principles of Christianity are clearly present, but they are called by a different name. Others choose the path of clean fiction that holds up Godly ideals such as truth and choosing good over evil.

Though clearly seen in the speculative fiction realm, this conflict over whether Christian writers should write exclusively Christian fiction spans all genres. Even though this ideal isn't widely proclaimed in conferences and writing circles, it's damaging enough to warrant our attention.

There are two sides to this issue. The first is the writer who *feels* like this is the message when they attend Christian writer's conferences because every class is tailored to those who do write faith-based stories. No one has told them they must write faith-filled stories, but many classes speak of weaving in the message or staying true to our calling as faith-based writers.

In cases like this, the exclusion felt by the writer is partially self-inflicted. Christian writer's conferences are tailored to writers of Christian fiction and nonfiction. They are not general writing conferences for Christians. The difference is small but important.

As a faith-based writer, I can attend a general writing conference and learn a great deal. I can enjoy time with other authors while growing in my craft and understanding of the writing business. I cannot, however, expect to receive encouragement or instruction specific to my calling as an author of faith-based books. That is not the purpose of the general market conferences.

It is the drive behind a Christian writer's conference. When a Christian author who doesn't write specifically faith-based stories acknowledges this purpose before attending a conference, the writer can come in with a different perspective. The faith-focus of the instruction isn't there to shake a finger at them. It's there to serve the purpose of building up the type of authors the conference was designed for.

The second part of this issue stems from definitions and miscommunication. What is Christian fiction, and what makes a writer a Christian or faith-based author?

The answers vary widely. Some social media groups use publishing houses as their guidelines. If it is a Christian publishing house, then, by default, it is a Christian book. While this guideline seems fair, there is a growing trend in some Christian publishing houses to move away from overt mentions of faith.

I recently picked up a book looking for a faith message. The book, a popular one, was released by a well-known Christian publishing house. I'd read reviews about this author's other books, and they seemed to be on point where faith was concerned. I dove into the story, expecting to come away with my faith bolstered or even challenged.

Neither happened.

Throughout the story, I waited for the faith. Other than a child saying a prayer before mealtime, there was little to no talk of faith. The main character, who admitted her belief in God was shaky at best, didn't grow or change in her faith throughout the story. The little girl's outlook gave her something to think about, but by the end of the book, thinking was all she'd done. And very little of that.

Was this book Christian fiction? In the strictest of definitions, yes. It was published by a Christian publishing house. There were no themes in opposition to faith. And, yes, a child said a prayer.

Did I feel cheated out of what I was looking for in choosing that story? Yes.

What I read was a good, clean story. But it didn't feel like the Christian fiction I've come to love and look to in encouraging my faith. Though, I do enjoy characters who consider their faith in every situation of life, because I believe that's what we should all strive for, an author doesn't have to bash the reader over the head with God's truth. Subtlety is acceptable and even preferred over beating it into me as I read.

There is a popular fantasy author who accomplishes this with expert precision. A reader approaching her stories without faith will find rich tales of good and evil. They'll find encouragement to consider actions and consequences, right and wrong, and how to help others when opposition is strong.

When Christians pick up her books, they will find the same themes as those without faith. Their experience with the story, however, will be richer and more faith-building as they see the correlation between the author's world and the body of Christ clearly demonstrated. The ideas of abusing the gifts of God and choosing to use them for the betterment of all take shape.

This author doesn't paint faith with blatant brush strokes, but a reader who has a relationship with God will clearly see the biblically based message of challenge and hope within the story. Not once does the author mention God as we know Him. He doesn't even exist in the world she's created. Nevertheless, for the believing reader, God is evident on every page.

It's easy to see why defining Christian fiction is difficult. How can a fantasy that doesn't mention God be Christian fiction, while a book released by a Christian publisher where a child prays to God doesn't feel like Christian fiction?

Even readers of Christian fiction cannot agree on the subject. Some feel fantasy has no place as Christian fiction. Others feel if God isn't overtly mentioned on every page, if there is no salvation message, then a story fails to reach Christian standards. There are those who feel any nod to God and faith at all, even in question, tips the scale in favor of a book being labeled Christian fiction.

The wide range of books offered by various Christian publishing houses indicates that there may not be an industry standard we can look to for a final answer. However, for the sake of this book, we will define Christian writing as any work that points to God and His truths, either overtly or allegorically. Christian writing is approached from a Christian worldview and does not oppose biblical truth.

Now that we've made the Christian writing definition as clear as mud, let's tackle the Christian author. A slight rewording can easily bring clarity to whether an author is a Christian author. It may seem like semantics, but in a discussion where hurt and discouragement have injured writing friends, it is important.

Is the writer a Christian? Do they have a personal relationship with God through Jesus Christ? While we can only take our friends at their word on the answers, if they are, then they are Christian writers. They are Christians who write.

But their stories lack a faith element. How can I call them Christian writers?

I can do so because, in this instance, calling them Christian writers has nothing to do with their content. It's about who they are, not what they write. Now, if I asked if they're authors of Christian books or faith-based books, the answer may be different. That phrasing references the works, not the state of the author.

Understand that when readers and those in the publishing industry reference Christian authors, they use the term interchangeably with authors of Christian books. This is not going to change, and whether it feels exclusionary or not, we need to accept the way it is. For the sake of our discussion, though, we need to acknowledge the difference.

And that brings us back to the original "rule": Christian writers must write Christian content. On the surface, this seems to make perfect sense. Using Christian writers synonymously with writers who are Christians, we find where this idea breaks down.

Writers who are Christians must write faith-based content.

A few cringed reading that sentence, while others adamantly nodded. Why do some insist that Christians who write must release only faith-based content?

It is an attempt to make everything we do "glorify God" as scripture commands in 1 Corinthians 10:31. If God has given the talent for writing and the passion to use the talent, then shouldn't we honor God with those blessings by turning on a floodlight of faith into the dark world through our writing?

Yes.

And no.

Yes, we should always honor God with what we write. Does this mean each story or book is a compilation of faith? No.

Before you run me out of town, let me clarify. Does your Christian mailman always engage in conversations of faith with you as he delivers your mail? What about your auto mechanic? Does he always pray over your car, asking God to help him find what's wrong and fix it? What about the teenager from the youth group who bags your groceries? Does she pray over you as she stuffs your sourdough bread into a bag or offer you an encouraging verse as she tells you good-bye?

We don't require Christians in other professions to focus their work on the gospel, and we shouldn't require it of authors, either. God has called some of us into the Christian publishing arena, but we must trust that God is also leading our Christian writer friends who create wholesome, clean stories for others to enjoy without an overt faith message.

While the belief that Christian authors should only write Christian stories is not a requirement we should adhere to, the heart of those who feel this way may be in the right place. Why would a Christian accept this idea?

Many reasons may exist. Some have little to no merit. Legalistic ideals that, like the Pharisees' proclamations, only serve to bring guilt to those who fail and puff up those who give in to the demand fall into this category. But there is one valuable reason we should give our attention—glorifying God.

We are called to glorify God in all we do. This is scriptural truth. Therefore, some people reason that a Christian writer must write Christian works. While it is true that a faith-laced story can bring glory to God and point others to the hope we have in Jesus, writing Christian stories and books is not the only way to accomplish this goal.

Bringing God glory through our lives and honoring Him and His gifts has as much to do with our attitudes as our actions. While writers who choose to write without a faith element may not have the same ministry aspect to their writing, there are still scriptural guidelines that promote giving God glory through their work.

*Bringing God glory through our lives and honoring Him and His gifts has as much to do with our attitudes as our actions.*

If you are an author of faith-based books, please do not skim through the following scriptures. They may give the writer of clean fiction a scriptural guide, but they also serve as an attitude check for those who write faith-based books. Even as a believer who writes clean stories can bring God glory, a writer of faith-based books can do so without God receiving the glory.

- Do we recognize our gifts and talents are from God? (James 1:17)
- Is our attitude about writing one of humility and serving others above self? (Philippians 2:3)
- Do we regularly seek God's plan and purpose for our writing? (Jeremiah 29:11)

Scriptural guidelines go beyond shaping our attitudes. While authors of faith may not always write books that specifically draw others to God, we must be vigilant not to lead readers away from His truths, either. Books that present a worldview as good or desirable in opposition to a scriptural worldview are akin to teaching readers that ungodly ideals are acceptable.

In our daily lives, we wouldn't tell our loved ones that sinful living is appropriate because that isn't true. The words we write have the same power as those we speak, and some would argue they own more power and reach more people. Readers are influenced by ideas presented in our writing as much as they're entertained by our stories. For example, studies have shown readers are more empathetic because they've virtually spent time in another person's shoes.

If we present ideas and beliefs as true and right that are against our faith and faith values, we do a disservice to our readers and to God. At this point, it would be tempting to dive into another list of dos and don'ts, giving specifics of what God deems acceptable or not. Yet while there are many black-and-white subjects in scripture, many fall into shades of gray.

This is where we look to principles in scripture and rely on the Holy Spirit's nudge inside us as our guide to employing what we learn. Again, we find ourselves in a place not where we ask, "How far is too far to go in my writing?" But rather, "How can I bring the most honor to God's name through my writing?"

I won't share a list of rules we must adhere to, but I will share a list of scriptures that can serve as guide in determining what subjects, actions, and words we want to include in our writing. At the least, I suggest coming back to this list any time you face the question, "Should I write this?"

Does what you're considering violate any of the principles? Is there another way to accomplish the same goal without toeing the line? Can you, without conviction from the Holy Spirit, write what you want to write in the way you plan to write it?

Ideally, I encourage using the list to determine in advance the lines you will not cross in your writing. Not only will pre-established boundaries free you from having to agonize over every new idea, they can also help keep you on track in your writing. No one wants to waste time with a story they determine is not one they should be writing after already having written several chapters.

- Philippians 4:19—Do I look to the world and its accolades to supply my needs or do I look to God for approval and supply of my needs?
- Hebrews 10:24-25—Does my writing stir up love and good deeds in others or encourage selfish thoughts or attitudes?
- John 2:15—Does my writing stir people up to love the world or the things of the world?
- Philippians 4:8—Does my writing reflect attitudes of honesty, justice, purity, and virtue?

- Galatians 5:19-21—Does my writing encourage or present as right and good the works of the flesh?
- 1 Corinthians 10:14—Does my writing glorify the pursuit of false gods or idols?
- Colossians 3:8, Ephesians 4:29, and Matthew 12:36—Are the words I write angry, slanderous, crude, or filthy? Or do they help and encourage others like a gift?

ACTION STEP

Prayerfully consider what you write and why. Listen for God's leading, even if it is different from what you expected to hear. Let the Holy Spirit guide you in defining your writing and your audience. Meditate on the above scriptures, asking God to show you truth and convict you where you may have veered off course. Use this time with God to develop a game plan for how you will handle sensitive subjects before the world comes knocking at your door, demanding its way.

# 8

# WRITE WHAT YOU KNOW

Write what you know. This rule seems reasonable and beneficial. Who better to explain the depth of loss faced when a child dies than a mother who has lived despite that heartache? Can a big city girl who's never left her concrete jungle be as nuanced in her descriptions of life on a working cattle ranch?

This rule seems like a no-brainer. Of course, you should only write about those things you've experienced for yourself. And yet ...

- Tolkien never traveled to the shire.
- C.S. Lewis never fell through a portal into a magical world.
- Liz Curtis Higgs never walked the moors of Scotland in the 1790s.
- Lori Wick wasn't a member of the British peerage in the 1800s.

None of these authors knew, in the experiential sense, what they were writing about. Yet, their works are beloved by readers. They've captured not only the imaginations but the hearts of readers across generations. They've encouraged readers to examine their lives and their faith in new ways. They've shown readers far-off times and places. They've taught readers about people they could never meet and even allowed readers to learn about themselves in the process.

These authors have accomplished all this without once living what they're writing. What happened to the write-what-you-know rule? Were these authors simply proficient enough to ignore it? Or is there a deeper principle we can cling to in our writing that allows us to write about whatever topic, place, or people catch our imagination?

Broken down to its most basic reason, writing what you know ensures two things in your writing: truth and realism. Even in their fantastical worlds, Tolkien and Lewis's themes, characters, and morals ring true. One can walk away from their stories feeling as if they could stroll through Middle Earth or find a lamppost in a wood inside a wardrobe. Even more impressive is being able to leave these imaginative stories with a stronger sense of self and the human condition.

 *Broken down to its most basic reason, writing what you know ensures two things: truth and realism in what you write.*

How did they accomplish such realism and truth in stories about made-up times, places, and people? How do historical writers deal with pasts they've had no part in? And can we as writers veer from the path of what we know in our writing without sacrificing truth and realism?

These examples show us it is possible to honor the heart of the write what you know rule while still taking the readers down paths we've never personally walked. We simply must put in the work to ensure we are true to the times, places, and themes in our work.

For nonfiction writers, this may look a bit different. I cannot write a book touting a faith I haven't personally experienced. Truth, in the case of nonfiction, is not relative. Failure to realize this can cause pain and damage the readers' faith.

When I was a child, there was a popular Christian comedian who spoke all around the country. While laced with humor, he shared his very powerful testimony. He'd been delivered from Satanism and had many life-changing experiences. The depth of faith he exhibited was an inspiration. His messages always ended with a call to accept Christ. The altar was full at every show.

Imagine his fans' surprise when the truth was revealed. This man's testimony was a lie. He'd not experienced half of what he shared with the audiences. While engaging and humorous, his stories, told as truth, were fabrications. My own faith was rooted deeply enough to avoid becoming the collateral damage of his failure. My heart hurt for those who came to know Jesus through this man's testimony only to find out the story that prompted their faith was false.

How many turned away after discovering the truth? How many believed they'd been duped into believing yet another lie, this one about God's saving love? How many used this man's failure as the final nail in the coffin of the church and faith? After all, if church people would lie like that, what kind of God must God be?

More mature believers can usually take a more balanced approach to these situations. New believers are often gutted by such scandals. As authors, especially in nonfiction genres, we are teachers. The calling to teach is one held to a high standard in scripture.

Nonfiction authors may easily see the correlation between their writing and teaching. Yet fiction authors, especially those who write faith-based stories, are not immune to the scriptural standards set apart for teachers. The themes we include in our stories, the scriptures, and the lessons our characters learn are meant to impact those reading our books. In this, and in our presentation of a faith-filled life, we are teachers too. Even those who choose not to write faith-based fiction have a level of responsibility to refrain from presenting as worthy and true worldviews that are in opposition to their faith.

James 3:1 presents a warning to those who teach. This verse encourages us to thoughtfully consider teaching because of the higher standard of judgment those who teach will face. Going along with this idea is an admonition in Mark 9:42, stating a person would be better off drowned than leading a child astray through their teachings.

This is a bold statement, but it highlights how seriously God takes the presentation of truth. As Christian authors, part of writing what we know from a spiritual aspect is studying the Word in context and weighing each idea against the entirety of scripture. Prayer for God to reveal truth to our hearts and guide us in our writing is always a great way to begin.

While we do have to know the truths we present, remember, "Knowing is half the battle." A half-fought fight does not yield the best results. The other part of writing what we know is taking the truths we know from scripture and living them daily.

The comedian I listened to in my childhood promised hope and love, but he left chaos and disappointment in his wake. The words he spoke of God and scripture were true. Other evangelists and speakers have shared similar truths without negative results. Why were the same words so damaging coming from this man?

At that time, he failed to live the truths he preached. No one expected perfection from him, but his lifestyle stood in direct opposition to the lessons he shared. Though there are many scriptures regarding living what you teach, about the hypocrisy of the religious leaders and the damage they caused, and about applying what you learn from the Word, one scripture sums them all up in a simple way we can all understand. James 1:22 states, *"But prove yourselves doers of the word, and not merely hearers who delude themselves."*

The whys and hows are covered in more detail in the verses following and preceding this one, but this truth is enough. We are to live what we learn. And like King David, when we fail at the task, we repent, make amends, and keep going. In doing this, others see authenticity in us and know the messages we present are true and applicable.

Growing in our relationship with God and understanding and applying His Word is how Christian authors respect the spiritual meaning behind "write what you know."

We strive for the same in the physical side of our writing. At one time, writing about people, places, and times we'd never experienced was incredibly difficult. Even at the time I was in school, research was painstakingly slow. If we couldn't visit a place we wanted to write about, we had one recourse—the library. Once there, we had to search the card catalog and find the proper books hiding in the labyrinth of shelves. Worse than the card catalog was scouring the microfiche. I'm sure many people ended up with eyeglass prescriptions due to eye strain caused by looking at those things!

Today, writers have a wealth of information at their fingertips. An author writing about faraway places can virtually visit using computer programs and real-time satellite images. Issues we've never faced and occupations we've never held can be researched for authenticity. Writers can learn whether cars were painted blue in the 1920s with a few clicks of a mouse and some well-chosen search terms.

With in-depth resources available twenty-four hours a day, seven days a week, it's much easier for something we don't know to become something we do know, at least on a surface level. Those last two words hold the great obstacle for writers in writing what they know. Surface level may work for the average Joe reader who has never been to England during the Victorian era, but what about the one who studied the period in college? Generic descriptions may be fine for someone who has never visited that random small town in Nebraska where your story is set. But those who live in the town will know there has never been an ice cream shop on the corner of Fifth and Main.

But what about poetic license? It is fiction, after all.

We can take some license with elements of our fictional stories. I never reference real churches in my stories, especially if they are having issues in my narrative. And I may add a business or two that isn't really in the town where my story is set. After all, businesses change almost daily. But I try to incorporate the feel of the town, true-to-life descriptions of the area, a few staples of the town, and the attitudes of the real community in the story.

When writing historical stories that include real people, honoring the "write what you know" ideal involves getting to know the people as best we can. Reading biographies and articles about those people can give writers a clearer image of the complexities of characters who are more than just words on a page. They were real, living people who shaped the times they lived in.

In my historical novel set in the 1920s in Harrisburg, Illinois, I not only researched businesses present at the time but also read several books about events in the area that had no direct correlation to my story. These books provided a clearer picture of the attitudes and events that shaped life in the town at that time. They also gave me insight into the complicated attitudes prevalent in the area and the world of gangsters in southern Illinois, especially the life of Charlie Birger.

Though he never spoke a word in my story, this gangster was a major player in the history of parts of southern Illinois, and his deeds shaped the events in the lives of my characters. Researching him and the area made it possible to flesh out my setting, characters, and plot in realistic ways to bring real life to my story. In this way, I fulfilled the task of writing what I knew, although I never lived it.

Research is necessary when writers want to write about subjects, times, or places they haven't experienced first-hand. Reliable research is vital.

The invention of the internet and the prevalence of information available through a simple search might seem like the holy grail for writers. An internet search can provide all we need, but the abundance of information can also be a Pandora's Box for those who do not understand how to use it wisely.

With one touch, thousands of sources are instantly available. However, as authors attempting to write what we know, it's important to realize not all sources are good sources. Is the article you're using to shape your character's view of depression written by an average Joe or a mental health professional? Is the study you referenced informal, or was care given to ensure the results stand up to scientific scrutiny? Have you inadvertently chosen a satire site or gossip rag instead of a trustworthy news site? When were the articles and books you're using written? Is the material outdated?

Reliable online or physical research is the first step in keeping everything we write true to life. But it is only one step. We have resources readily available to us that our writing predecessors couldn't fathom.

When writing about a group of people or issues we have not personally dealt with, sensitivity readers can go a long way toward filling in the blanks of what we don't know. Whether your book features other cultures or sensitive topics, those who have experienced what you're writing about can be a great asset.

I grew up in a small midwestern town in southern Illinois. The area is rural, with a lot of farming and coal mining. Everyone knew everyone else where I grew up. Though it wasn't Mayberry, sitting on the front porch chatting with those walking by was not an unusual occurrence.

This is my experience. If I want to write about growing up in inner-city Chicago, I can use reliable research as a starting point to shape my narrative. However, once the story begins taking shape, I can go a step further in my quest for authenticity. I can reach out to sensitivity readers who understand the people and attitudes prevalent in inner-city Chicago.

As with research, not all sensitivity readers are created equal. I have friends who grew up in the suburbs of Chicago. While they have more experience with the inner city than I do, they have still not experienced growing up *in* inner-city Chicago. They would not make adequate sensitivity readers for my book.

There are great variations in experience within a single area, culture, or situation. Each family and individual will interpret and react to the same stimuli differently. Having multiple sensitivity readers allows the author to get a feel for what seems most prevalent in each case.

Trainings are another great way to turn an unknown into something familiar. I've never investigated a crime, and I doubt my hours watching police procedurals are a reliable source of information. There are, however, classes I could take to help me understand what it feels like to shoot a gun or how to lift a fingerprint properly.

Community colleges are a wonderful source of classes on a variety of topics at a reasonable price. Conferences, those for writers and those in the field you need to research, are another wonderful way to increase your knowledge on needed subjects.

Even if hands-on training is not feasible, writers are not without options. Interviews with professionals, people impacted by various issues, and those who have lived in the time periods you are writing about are more than valuable for attaining the facts you need. They also provide real-life insight into thoughts, feelings, and lessons learned.

When writers use reliable research, sensitivity readers, training, and interviews, they can move beyond the scope of what they know first-hand and still honor the meaning behind writing what they know.

* * *

ACTION STEP

Consider the subjects, places, times, and people you write about, especially in reference to your work in progress or any manuscripts you haven't published yet. Which of these do you have personal experience with? Which ones are foreign to you? While you may not be able to attain first-hand knowledge, determine the best ways to honor the goal of writing what you know. Craft a plan to incorporate these ways into your writing and take the first steps to ensure your writing stays true to the reality it's supposed to portray.

# 9

# PLOTTERS, PANTSERS, AND PLANTSERS ... OH, MY!

If you read the introduction, you know this rule is near to my heart. It's the one that almost ended it all for my writing career. (Now, aren't you sorry you didn't read the Introduction? Go ahead. Flip back to it. I'll wait.) And while the consensus on this rule is shifting, leaving it more principle than rule, many of the tools, tips, and methods touted by writers today still promote this idea in practice, if not in words.

For those unfamiliar with the terminology, plotting is mapping out your story—the characters, setting, obstacles, and major details of a story—before beginning to write. Pantsing is the practice of simply writing and seeing where the words lead. You'll often hear these authors say things like, "I was so surprised where the character took me ..." as if they aren't the ones in control of the story. And then there are the plantsers. These authors employ a blend of plotting and pantsing. They aren't as meticulous with their pre-writing work as a true plotter, but they also aren't as willing to follow wherever the story leads as a pantser.

For many years, as it was in the days when I began writing, plotters were king. The plotter's golden rule was announced in every workshop and conference. To write well-crafted stories with strong characters and plotlines woven tight enough to carry water without spilling a drop, a writer must plot out their book from beginning to end. This must take place before a single word of prose is written.

Those not wired this way cringe at the thought. Can we write using intricate plot points we've previously developed? Most of us can if we put our minds to it. For writers who grew up writing five-paragraph essays, the tools of preplanning were drilled into us starting in junior high, if not sooner.

Choose your topic. Develop three arguments that support your theme. Introduce the theme and three supportive statements along with a concluding sentence to transition into the first body paragraph. After you've expounded on the three points, craft a strong concluding paragraph to wrap it all up with a bow.

Before we ever wrote a word, the essays were outlined. In fact, the outlines generally required teacher approval before we could move on to the actual writing.

Though used for nonfiction, this was the first introduction many of us received to the wonderful world of plotting. As a student learning how to transform sentences into paragraphs and papers, I easily adjusted to this method of writing. However, as I grew in my skills and my understanding of who I am as a writer, I branched out into more creative presentations of the material.

The ability to use a method doesn't equal the method being natural to you or the most productive for you. This lesson came early as I worked on writing assignments. I found myself writing complete papers. Then, to meet the grading criteria, I would go back and make an outline from my finished project to turn in for the pre-planning portion of my grade. And because teachers wanted to see earlier drafts, I would mess up some of the sentences and wording from my final draft on an extra copy. As each due date arrived, I turned in the required portion while having the finished assignment at home. I used the same approach in my creative writing.

I didn't realize it then, but my writing nature was coming out in force. And while I can plot a story, and have done so a few times in my writing career, it is not my preference. I feel stifled in my creativity and slowed in my progress when under the pressure of plotting.

If you are a plotter, there's great news. There is no shortage of plotting methods and tools. With a bit of research, you should be able to find the right one for your writing style.

The *Save the Cat* method is a popular plotting tool. It's used across genres with success. Written by screenwriter Blake Snyder, *Save the Cat* breaks down the screenwriting process into fifteen story beats or plot points and their respective timing in the story being told.

Mr. Snyder's focus was on screenwriting, but the ideas he presents are applicable to storytelling of any sort. However, if adjusting to fit is not in your wheelhouse, Jessica Brody has applied Snyder's understanding of these elements of storytelling and written *Save the Cat Writes a Novel*, which focuses on the same ideas tailored to novel writing.

The Hero's Journey is another method. This one was developed by Joseph Campbell, who noticed a pattern in the way mythology tells stories. This method works across genres, including those not related to mythological type stories. Instead of plot points or story beats, the story is broken into different stages of the protagonist's journey or reaching his goal.

The Plot Pyramid or Freytag's Pyramid may be the most familiar to those just beginning their writing journey. Though I don't recall it having a name in my elementary school years, I do remember the visual of the pyramid with the action building to a peak before dropping down into the resolution. This is a basic plotting device without a lot of the extra details included in the other methods, but it is a useful tool, nonetheless.

There are many other methods a writer can try on for fit. The one most of us probably started with during school is the Three Act Structure. It taught us that a story is very simply made of a beginning, middle, and end. As we grew, setup, confrontation, and resolution may have replaced those terms.

If you're looking for something more involved, Dan Harmon adapted The Hero's Journey into the Story Circle which focuses on the cyclical nature of story. There is also the 27 Chapter Method by Kat O'Keefe, which divides twenty-seven chapters into three acts. The Plot Dot by Derek Murphy is another template many authors employ.

In addition to these general methods, outlines, and templates are genre-specific tools. For romance, an author might choose *Romancing the Beat: Story Structure for Romance Novels (How to Write Kissing Books)* by Gwen Hayes or Susan May Warren's *How to Write a Brilliant Romance,* which includes plotting the story but also dives deeper into other aspects of story creation related to romances. Non-romance writers may find beneficial information in these methods, but they are formatted to ensure each expected piece of the romance puzzle is included in a writer's story.

There are two important considerations when deciding which method is right for you. The first is an understanding that while we may be Christian authors, some who have created these methods do not necessarily share our faith. Their books, blogs, websites, and videos may be full of helpful information, but they may also include language you find offensive or examples of scenes from books that are not clean fiction.

Second, understand that this is not a comprehensive list of plotting methods, but it does give those interested in incorporating plotting into their writing a place to start. Though different, many of the methods will share specific ideas or timing of when events should happen. It is important to note that different genres and even some publishers have specific outlines of how they want a story to progress. Save yourself time in rewrites. Research your genre and publisher expectations prior to finishing your manuscript.

For me, freedom came with hearing there was another way. I could write without an emphasis on plotting beforehand. But with freedom comes added responsibility. There are good reasons for plotting, and writers need to consider them.

While I won't say plotting is mandatory in certain genres, those like mystery and suspense receive extra help from knowing what's going to happen before it takes place. It's difficult to weave red herrings and subtle, yet believable, clues into a story if you don't know who the culprit is before you start writing. It's also difficult to avoid littering your story with fake clues that don't lead anywhere or have any relevance to the outcome. These can leave the reader frustrated with your writing, and frustrated readers are not repeat readers.

Aside from the special needs of mystery and suspense stories, plotting provides many valuable safeguards for our writing. Plotting helps writers see how all the moving parts of their story work together to make the whole. It can show them the sagging middle that needs shored up. Or it can help them avoid a rushed ending. Plotting can show not only the plot holes but also the rabbit trails that should be cut to make the story stronger and keep the action moving forward.

These benefits are at the heart of the push to plot. However, striving for stronger stories doesn't have to mean accepting plotting as a way of life. There are many ways to make sure your story is as strong as it can be, even if you choose not to plot.

*Striving for stronger stories doesn't have to mean accepting plotting as a way of life.*

One way to strengthen your writing is through reading, and reading across multiple genres is even better. Not only do those who read have stronger vocabularies, which means a greater potential to use language that works well for your story, but they can also grow in creativity and their ability to think critically. Better creativity and critical thinking skills can help writers see where something isn't working in their stories and brainstorm ways to fix it.

Reading also allows writers to experience elements of language and how they work together. Employing that knowledge in their writing helps strengthen their manuscripts. With exposure to writing styles and different author voices, a writer can develop their own.

If you'd like to know more about the benefits of reading to learn, here is a link to an article on the subject. While the information is commonly known and spoken of, the article is a quick read and addresses additional benefits of reading you may find interesting. https://www.95percentgroup.com/insights/reading-importance.

Remember, though, not all reading is created equal. Consistently read stories written at a level you strive for in your own writing. If your main reading diet consists of books where the authors exhibit bad writing habits, you may pick up some of those bad habits as well. Quality is the aim of plotting. Even if we choose not to plot, we still desire our work to be high quality.

A second method for keeping the heart of the plotting message without adopting it completely is plantsing. A mix of plotting and pantsing can help keep the story hole-free and freely flowing. And it doesn't have to take place before writing the story.

Though I've never heard this term before, we're going to call this hybrid post-plotting. I regularly engage in post-plotting. As I finish a scene or a chapter, I write down the details in a separate list. I include when the actions take place, including what time of year, the month, and the days of the week, if possible. I also write down the basic actions of my characters and important plot points that took place.

Having these details at my fingertips as I continue to write can help me see where I might be veering off point. They can show me chapters that may need strengthening. If my synopsis of the chapter is blah, I need to punch up the emotion or conflict. There are even times when I read through the barest details of what I've already written that something new jumps out at me. Suddenly, I know where the story is going or understand a character's motivations in ways that were previously unclear.

Even if you never touch a pen or keyboard to outline your plot, there are still helpful ways to ensure your characters are strong and plot holes are patched before publishing. In addition to sensitivity readers, look for alpha and beta readers for your work.

Alpha readers are some of the first people to see your work-in-progress. They can include critique partners, your local writing group, or even friends who are also avid readers of the genre in which you write. These early readers may receive your manuscript piece by piece, or perhaps they will only read the portions of the book you feel may need shoring up.

While those who share an affinity for your preferred genre are ideal, great feedback can come from those outside your genre at this stage. However, not all genres are created with the same focus. Weigh all feedback against what is expected in your genre to determine which thoughts should be given the most attention as you rewrite.

Critique partners can be found through writing groups you participate in. In person or online, critique partners are a valuable resource in your writing. But remember, it's better to give than to receive. Make sure you're giving as much to your critique partner as they give to you.

Beta readers read your manuscript earlier than the general public, but these people will read your work after it's completed. They provide feedback on the reader's experience. Were they confused by something? Did they feel your writing was missing vital information? Did everything flow well for them?

The feedback you receive from beta readers will help you further smooth out rough spots in your writing before sending it on to editors for professional-level feedback. At this stage, it is important to have avid readers in your target audience serving this function. Those widely read in your genre will give the most usable feedback.

There may be crossover in your alpha and beta readers. Alpha readers and beta readers can be found in writing groups, but they can be found in reader groups as well. Avid readers are always eager for ways to get their hands on new books. Take care, though. Careful selection of your alpha readers is important. If you've tried someone, and you find their feedback is not on par with that offered by others, don't feel obligated to keep sending them more of your work.

Your time is valuable. So is theirs. Don't forget to show your appreciation for the time these early readers have given to you. A card or a thoughtful thank-you email can go a long way in making each early reader feel you appreciate them and their efforts. Don't take their work or expertise as avid readers for granted. Their time with your manuscript can help strengthen your writing, whether you're a plotter, pantser, or plantser.

It's also important to remember that just because you don't use a plotting method before you begin writing doesn't mean it's useless for you. In school, we learned to check our subtraction with addition. Work back through the problem from the other direction. In some math classes, we may even have been required to check our work and show the process we used.

We can apply the same principle to our writing. Go back through your story. Did you hit the fifteen plot points from *Save the Cat*? Is your hero's journey complete with each step along the way? Even the most die-hard pantsers can check their work using one of these plotting methods after the writing is done. Doing so allows writers to see where their stories excel and where they may need to fill a plot hole before it jars the reader out of the story.

ACTION STEP

> Are you a plotter, pantser, or plantser? Be aware that this can change as we develop our writing styles. Have you tried any of the plotting methods mentioned in this chapter? Research each

one to determine if one is right for you. No matter your plotting habits, make a list of groups you could reach out to for alpha and beta readers and, if needed, sensitivity readers. Also, develop a list of authors in your chosen genre who inspire you to write at their level of expertise. If you've read all their books, ask other readers for similar recommendations.

## 10

# GETTING THE WORDS OUT

You have your story plotted, or at the very least, you have a starting point. You've dedicated time to write and found a place that works for your writing needs. Now, it's time to get the words on the paper or the screen, as the case may be.

The process of transforming thoughts into words and stringing them together into coherent sentences and paragraphs may have less-defined rules than other elements of the writing process, but this doesn't mean there is less to consider. What the writing world lacks in rules regarding this, it more than makes up for in writing methods and tools.

I've met several writers who choose to handwrite their manuscripts for the first draft. I cannot imagine doing this. Being left-handed, my handwriting quickly devolves into sloppiness that even I cannot interpret. And the hand cramps! No, I will happily leave hand-written drafts to others.

But do I type in Microsoft Word? What about in Google Docs? Do I dip my toe into the Scrivener pool? What about LivingWriter, Storyist, or a host of other software products that help you plan or write your book? Most importantly, what is the difference in each of these programs?

It's important to note that Microsoft Word and Google Docs are word processors. Next to some of the other programs out there, they are glorified typewriters. You can type the words, save them, and even format them, but they don't include a lot of the extras the writing programs include.

These two do offer a few bells and whistles, like spelling and grammar checks. And you can search your documents for specific words or phrases. You can even find synonyms without having to open a search engine. And, if you type according to the specifications of your publisher, your manuscript will be formatted properly without having to export it from a separate program to make it publisher-ready. But if you're looking for something to keep all the details of your story in one place, these are not going to cut it.

Storyist, LivingWriter, Scrivener, and other programs created specifically for writers are different. They are a one-stop shop for all your writing needs. Each one offers a variety of elements to enhance your writing time.

Many of these programs have blueprints or templates built in for the different plotting methods we discussed earlier. Plug your information straight into those blueprints and keep them handy as you write so you don't miss anything important or get off track. You can also create character sketches using many of these programs. Every detail of your character, including inspiration photos, is kept together for quick reference. Your research notes and maps for the story's setting can be stored as well.

Each program will also offer different levels of AI (Artificial Intelligence) help. Please note that I am not endorsing the use of AI in the creation of your manuscript. I have convictions on what is and is not ethical regarding AI and creative pursuits, but this book does not deal with that subject. This is about tools available to writers, and AI is one of those tools built into many of the writing programs we use, even in Microsoft Word at a basic level. Therefore, it should be included as a writing tool.

Need help with your writing goals? Many of these programs include goal trackers and allow writers to see the progress they're making. If you don't want to use one of these more in-depth programs but still want help tracking your writing goals, there are free programs like WriteTrack that allow you to map out your goals based on the date you want to finish your project and which days are high or low productivity days for you.

After attending several workshops that praised Scrivener, I jumped on the bandwagon. I loved the concept—all my notes, photos, research, and timelines in one convenient place. Pictures of my characters uploaded so I can look to them for inspiration as I write. It sounded like a little piece of heaven to me. However, a little internal nudge told me not to jump into the deep end with my bank account before I'd tested this miracle through the free trial.

I'm glad I listened.

I'm tech-capable but not really a tech person. I learn programs I need and usually only enough to do what I set out to do. When I need to learn more of the program's capabilities, I will. Until then, learning only what I need seems like the best option.

Scrivener and I didn't get along well. The promised piece of heaven felt more like time in purgatory. There was so much to learn to unleash all the program's wonderful features. I felt like I was spending more time trying to find things I'd previously saved or figuring out how to reorder notes I'd added than I was writing. Not fully comfortable with all the ins and outs, I struggled. I refreshed myself with how-to classes and videos. My journey with Scrivener did not improve.

Determined to accomplish writing during my writing times and having given myself adequate time to learn the program, I abandoned ship. I arrived at the place where I could use it, but it still seemed to bog me down.

If you find yourself trying and failing to implement a popular writing tool in your writing, you're not alone. They aren't for everyone any more than a traditional model of education is for everyone. We're all different. We learn in unique ways, and we work in equally unique ways.

 *If you find yourself trying and failing to implement popular writing software in your writing, you're not alone.*

Are those who find more frustration than success with writing programs doomed to a writing life void of order and inspiration? Not at all.

While plotting tools are one of the perks of these programs, we've already discussed the heart of plotting. If you need to, review the last chapter to refresh yourself on the options available to you in that area.

What about the timelines, research, and inspirational photographs? What about the family trees and notecards that allow you to shuffle ideas around until they fit together seamlessly? And why do writing programs include those to begin with?

Scrivener, LivingWriter, and other writing programs are about organization and keeping all the materials for your writing in one convenient place. They are about allowing writers to be their most productive selves. The less time we spend looking back through notebooks or flipping through folders to find out what color our main character's eyes are, the more words we can get on the page.

If you're a more visual or tactile learner and these programs aren't working, there are still ways to increase your productivity through organization. One of the elements touted by users of these programs is the ability to create note cards for scenes, chapters, plot points, or characters. But these are *virtual* notecards. For those who don't adapt well to the virtual offerings, we can use physical notecards.

With an index card box and dividers, you can quickly and easily organize your cards into individual story parts. Any time you need to flesh out a detail, pop open the box and flip to the correct section. If you're even more visually oriented, choose a package of multi-colored cards instead of standard cards. Assign a different color for each element you want to track.

If it stifles your creative process to flip through a box every time you need information, consider alternative methods of organizing your notecards. A corkboard is a great option. Whether you mount it on the wall or leave it unattached and able to move to each workspace with you, a large board can keep your information front and center. Some may tack strings to the wall and clip cards to the string with clothespins, allowing them to shift cards around as they brainstorm.

I've come to recognize my personality preferences hinder me from using the popular, yet somewhat complex, writing programs many authors adore. I need the easiest, quickest method to locate my information with as little interruption to my writing as possible. This also precludes the use of notecards that must be leafed through or kept in close proximity. I'm too distractible. Every moment away from my computer screen is a moment that the temptation to do other activities can strike.

I found an alternative to both writing programs and cards, which keeps the information I need readily available, easy to find with a quick glance, and appeals to my desire for color and variation. Magnetic dry-erase boards and a selection of colored markers are my tools of choice. My boards are fixed to the wall across from my desk, but if I didn't have a set office space, they could easily be made portable.

One board is reserved for my heroine and one for my hero. Details about their physical descriptions, hobbies, jobs, spiritual lives, and personalities are added as I discover the information, the hero's information in one color and the heroine's in another.

My third board is dedicated to the setting, plot, and key timeline points. For my contemporary novels, this worked well. However, when I wrote my historical novel, I found adding the needed notes on historical information meant the board was too small. I had to modify my process. I did so with small posterboard sheets I tacked on the wall with the information that wouldn't fit on my whiteboards. Everything I need surrounds my space, and all I must do to find it is look up.

Whatever method you choose, take consistent advantage of its benefits. Like the writer's programs available, these tools can help lessen frustration in your writing time. Having everything you need in a set place and format that works for you is a great time saver and productivity encourager.

ACTION STEP

> Make a list of the different ways you've attempted to organize your writing information. Include everything from notebooks and folders to notecards to programs like Scrivener. Leave room to write down the pros and cons of each one. Did any leave you with greater frustration? Did you give yourself adequate time to learn and adapt to the program? Did any work for a time and then stop? Why did it stop? Is there a way to tweak the ones that once worked, allowing them to be beneficial once more? Can you take various successful elements and develop one system that works for you? Remember, if something stops working, it may be time to adjust your methods for a time. Adding flexibility and variation to your systems can be helpful to keep some people on track.

## 11

# CREATING CONVINCING CHARACTERS

Another important element in our writing processes is the creation of characters our readers connect with and come to seem like their next best friend. Writers make this possible through the creation of well-rounded characters.

Readers are not content with detailed physical descriptions of our heroes and heroines. While those details are important, they only scratch the surface. Readers want to know what motivates the people in our stories. And while not every minute detail of their lives should be included in our prose, we're told we, the authors, must know those details.

Authors must strike a balance between sharing and oversharing. Failure to achieve this balance can bog down the reader and convince them to stop turning pages. Most, if not all, of us have probably walked away from a book disappointed. The plot was engaging. We could picture the setting as if watching it on the big screen. The themes spoke to us on a personal level. Still, we're left feeling less than satisfied.

Why?

Because while the characters were fine, we didn't connect with them. We couldn't see ourselves in them or even walking beside them as a best friend. We finished three hundred pages without ever feeling like we truly knew the character. Maybe we weren't given enough insight into the inner workings of their minds to help us love them. Or it could be those little details that draw readers to characters didn't even exist in the author's mind. Whatever the reason, the character suffers, becoming flat and ineffective.

At the other end of the spectrum are authors who share too much. Too many quirks litter the page. Tired stereotypes fill the blanks reserved for the character's true personality, which should grow from their wounds and successes and experiences. These on and off the page details create a realistic character with gifts and flaws. They aid the author in ensuring their characters act "in character" in every situation.

They foster a connection for the reader. Kinship with the character, in turn, builds a connection between the reader and the overall story, keeping readers coming back for more.

*Compelling characters are key to drawing our readers in and keeping them eager to turn the pages.*

There's no question. Compelling characters are key to drawing readers in and keeping them eager to turn the pages. There are several schools of thought on accomplishing this goal. Don't worry. This chapter's Action Step will include a list of resources any author can use to understand how to develop compelling characters.

I remember exactly what I thought the first time I heard about the PDF for DiAnn Mills' Advanced Characterization Sketch during a conference workshop.

*Fifteen pages? There's no way.*

I knew I'd misheard. Only, as I opened my folder to the handouts, I realized it was true. DiAnn Mills uses a fifteen-page worksheet to flesh out her characters before she starts on chapter one. I'd always held her in great esteem, but understanding this part of her process elevated her even further in my eyes.

DiAnn uses this tool beautifully and with great success. Using both her character worksheet and plotting methods, DiAnn weaves wonderful tales of romantic suspense for her readers with characters so real they could sit beside us at the dinner table.

DiAnn's fifteen-page Advanced Characterization Sketch works. It's worked for her and for those she's taught in conferences and individually mentored. Her character development method covers physical, emotional, spiritual, and experiential details of her characters. Some of these details will end up on the page, but many are used behind the scenes to strengthen her characters. Openly written or unknown, each detail makes her characters who they are for the readers.

Author Brandilyn Collins takes a unique approach to creating characters. Hollywood shapes her character creation, in the form of lessons learned and adapted from the art of method acting many in the film industry embrace.

The basic concept of method acting, adopting the habits and mindsets of a character on and off camera throughout filming, is not new. We've read stories of strange things actors have done in the name of learning who their character is and transforming themselves into that person.

As film-goers, we may feel it's ridiculous. For those who don't accomplish their goal or who take it too far and end up hurting themselves or the production in their attempt, method acting becomes a weakness instead of a strength. However, there are those who excel at method acting, and their performances carry them all the way to the Oscars. For the length of the film, those actors seamlessly *become* the character they are portraying.

As authors, we don't need to become the characters in our books the same way actors do. This is good. We can move forward in creating stronger characters while avoiding the downfall of weird behavior that can happen when a method actor takes their role too far. Still, there is much we can learn, as Brandilyn did, from the process.

According to her, the method acting approach has seven characteristics that provide a great framework for creating characters. Each of these "secrets" helps authors realize the internal and external drives, actions, and beliefs that will make their characters come to life.

Personality quizzes are another tool many authors employ in deciding the ins and outs of their characters. Just as we discussed in Chapter Two the importance of knowing who and how God created you as a writer, it's equally important for the writer to know the who and how of their characters. Our characters are no different than us. Their personalities and experiences shape their actions and reactions.

As writers flesh out their characters' likes and dislikes, hobbies and occupations, they should also give time to the internal. Keeping our characters within the bounds of their personalities is important to keep them real and keep readers immersed in the world we've created. Our heroes and heroines should only act outside their nature when pushed there by someone or something in the story.

A sweet, quiet, people-pleaser who doesn't like to rock the boat won't suddenly spout off during a business meeting when she disagrees with her boss—at least not without good reason. Maybe this time, her boss has proposed something that goes strongly against a core value or need that your heroine has established as a line in the sand. Or maybe there is an outside factor that has created a time bomb of frustration in her, and his comments lit the fuse.

If our character acts out of character, they must have good reason. To recognize this, we must first recognize who our characters are. Only when we see our characters as clearly as we see ourselves (or sometimes more so) can we ensure they don't confuse or frustrate our readers with uncharacteristic behaviors.

When considering character development, overlap with plot is unavoidable. The plot and the character, even if the plot is externally driven, affect each other. The character's goal and reason for reaching that goal cannot be separated from the plot. They are inseparably tied together. For authors who desire realistic and fully formed characters, understanding what they want and why they want it is critical.

*GMC: Goal, Motivation, & Conflict* by Debra Dixon delves into the marriage of your character and the story's plot to create strong fiction. While not specifically focusing on character, it is the character's goal and motivation that fuel the GM portion of GMC.

When an author knows their characters' goals, motivations, and their personalities, the conflict portion of their story springs to life. Conflict is created when something stands in the way of our hero or heroine reaching their goal. The best roadblocks are those that are in direct opposition to who our characters are at their core.

Asking a character to do something outside their comfort zone, their personality, or their core beliefs creates the tension our stories need. The character must either grow in some needed area or find alternative ways to reach their goal without giving in to those demands against their beliefs.

Considering these principles, it's easy to see why knowing the nuances of our characters is vital, even details that readers never see. However, as the previous methods show, there isn't a one-size-fits-all approach to character creation.

I may never use the fifteen-page character profile DiAnn Mills created. I'd love to, but it's not in my personality to fill out so much paperwork. I'll probably never exclusively use Brandilyn's method-acting approach either. And while I'm a huge fan of personality studies, I have yet to take a personality quiz for my characters.

That said, I've gleaned a lot from DiAnn and Brandilyn's teachings. Both have excelled in the craft, and ignoring their expertise would be detrimental to my writing. Yet, instead of a rigid use of their systems, I adapt them to work for me.

My lack of physically taking a personality quiz for my characters doesn't mean I've ignored their personality principles in my character creation. Having studied and trained in personality systems, I've taken time to learn not only the basics of personality but also how experiences, upbringing, and societal norms can affect the natural bent of a person. I understand how personalities react under stress and when all in the world is in complete harmony. Having given time to this area of study, I can apply the principles without having to complete a personality quiz every time I create a character.

The heart of these character-creation methods is developing believable, well-rounded characters. Yet, if you can't follow one of these methods to the letter, there is still hope. Glean the principles from each system that resonate most with you. Then, put them into use in a way that makes sense for you.

For me, this looks like the two whiteboards on my office wall across from my desk. Remember, one is reserved for the hero, the other for the heroine. Each has an inspirational photo posted in the corner. This may be a generic photo from the internet or a specific actor or actress I feel fits the character I'm working on.

Even with the photo, I need quick descriptors. I add the character's physical traits to the board. From across the room, I may not be able to see the sea-green eyes of my leading man in the photo, but I can read the words.

In addition to physical traits, I add information about jobs, family, faith, personality, hobbies, and favorites to the board. The car the character drives and important events that shaped who they are both find a place on the board.

While my boards contain many of the same notes found on DiAnn Mills' characterization worksheet, others may be missing. Where her method is meant for pre-writing, my notes vary. I may only know some of the most important details from the beginning. They're added before I venture into the story. Others are added as I discover them during the writing process.

When I find myself in the middle of a scene, and my character needs to react to something, I can weigh each possibility against what I know about them from my character board. This helps me keep the character in line throughout the story.

This method also provides the why for each character. For example, if I know my heroine's boyfriend cheated on her, and her parents blamed her for his behavior, unless she's gone through some counseling, she will probably have trust issues and doubt herself. If my heroine was naturally self-assured before this, the trauma might cause a war within herself between what she knows is true versus what the situation feels like.

Whether you use a fifteen-page character worksheet, whiteboards, or keep your character information in a notebook or on notecards, honor the heart of character-creation methods. Your readers will be forever grateful for well-rounded characters they connect with on a personal level.

ACTION STEP

> Reflect on your method of character creation. Do you leave it up to chance or instinct? Are there any steps you take every time you create a new character? How well does this work for you in making memorable and realistic characters? Choose at least one of the following resources to deepen your understanding of character creation. Even if the specifics of the method don't pair well with your personality, stay alert for important principles and how you might modify them to work for you.
> 
> - *Exploring the Art of Character* by DiAnn Mills
> - *Getting into Character* by Brandilyn Collins
> - *GMC: Goal Motivation & Conflict* by Debra Dixon

- *Writing Unforgettable Characters: How to Create Story People Who Jump Off the Page* by James Scott Bell
- *How to Write Dazzling Dialogue* by James Scott Bell
- *Plot Versus Character: A Balanced Approach to Writing Great Fiction* by Jeff Gerke

# 12

# TRADITIONAL OR NOT AT ALL

You've spent the last weeks, months, or years writing. You've finally added *The End* to your manuscript. From the time the idea sprouted, you've known you wanted the world to read your book. Not wanting to assume, you've asked God if your plan is also His. You've received His green light.

Now what?

In the not-so-distant past, the answer would have been a resounding, "Traditional publishing only." The prevailing belief was that self-publishing gave the industry a bad name. The inferiority of the finished product discouraged people from reading any Christian books, and the general population already tended to think poorly of Christian books.

Times have changed, and so have many people's opinions of Christian publishing. There are still those who believe Christian books are inferior products. However, and this is simply my personal belief on the subject, I feel those people probably fall into two camps. Either they haven't had recent experience with Christian writing, or they simply have an issue with the Christian part of Christian publications.

- Do poorly written Christian books exist? Yes.
- Do poorly written mainstream and clean books exist? Yes.

A few minutes on the social media pages of mainstream bookstagrammers or booktokkers leave no doubt that poorly written is poorly written—genre doesn't matter. There are countless videos of people reading snippets of awkwardly worded descriptions and sentences. Many poke fun at over-the-top similes and metaphors sprinkled into the prose or point out overused tropes and tired character descriptors.

If it's not about the genre, then why do these poorly written books exist? Some, though not as many as in previous generations, would blame the world of indie publishing. Without the safeguards publishing houses put into place, the rigorous editing processes, and professional designers, the quality of books on the market is dismal.

Low-quality books, riddled with grammatical errors and dressed in less-than-professional covers, prompted the idea that self-published, commonly called indie-published, authors were less legitimate. They were the blight bringing down the reputation of the traditionally published author.

At its inception, self-publishing did allow poorly designed and written books to flood the market. Vanity presses promised to transform anyone willing to pay their fees into a published author. They still do. Some of these companies even promise professional editing for your book. The success with which they do this varies greatly.

One of the perks of the time we live in is the availability of computer programs anyone can use to aid in the creation of a self-published book that rivals those released by publishing houses. Another benefit is the ability to find the cover design, editing, and formatting help we need to create quality books with a few clicks of a mouse.

Advances like these have made quality self-publishing easier than ever before. This is great news for those who want to indie publish. Creating a professional book without going through a publishing house isn't impossible. In fact, with a little know-how, an investment of time and funding, and the internet, indie publishers can consistently produce quality books.

If both indie and traditional publishing can release award-winning, reader-loved, quality books, which way is the correct path for authors? As with many of the ideas we've discussed, there is no absolute answer. There are, however, some realities to consider and questions you should ask yourself. Before we look at those, let's return to the heart of the matter.

The reason people historically considered traditional publishing as the only legitimate path to becoming an author was because of the inferior quality material vanity presses often released. If we, as authors, seek to honor the heart of this concept, we must filter our publishing options and journey through this lens.

A desire for quality isn't about human pride. Although the growth and success of Christian publishing are affected by the quality of books on the market, the point isn't even safeguarding the reputation of Christian publishing. Scripturally, we are called to do our best in our work.

Colossians 3:23-24 states, *"Whatever you do, do your work heartily, as for the Lord rather than for men, knowing that from the Lord you will receive the reward of the inheritance."* While humans will be the ones reading what we write, the one we want to honor with our work is God. We've discussed bringing glory to God and honoring Him through the themes we write about, but those lessons also apply to the quality of our writing.

*We've discussed glorifying God and honoring Him through the themes we write about, but those lessons also apply to the quality of our writing.*

If we seek to honor God with our work, quality becomes even more important. Our God deserves our best. The most God-honoring answers to all questions we ask ourselves are the ones that allow us to publish quality, professional-grade books. The answers will be as varied as the authors writing the books.

Pray about each of the following questions. Be completely honest with yourself in the answers, even if you feel your answer isn't what it should be. When we know where our heart stands on a subject, we can ask God to show us how to bring it in line with His desires for us. Only continue reading after you've taken time with each question.

- Why are you considering indie/traditional publishing?
- What kind of budget is available?
- How technologically proficient are you?

*Why are you considering indie/traditional publishing?*

Is pride prompting your desire for a traditional publishing contract? If your internal dialogue tells you indie publishing is less prestigious or valid, it's possible pride is playing a role in your decision-making. The same could be said of one who feels indie publishing is the best way because no one else can present your words the way your words need to be presented.

Is a lack of patience pushing you toward indie publishing?

You've attended conferences and met with agents and publishers. Your book is finished. Early readers have sung its praises. You sent it to the publisher you spoke with at that one conference and were heartbroken when the rejection letter arrived. The publishing house doesn't want your book. You've already waited so long to see your words in print. Indie publishing is just as good as traditional, and you don't have to wait on someone else's acceptance.

Is your motivation grounded in having others do the undesirable tasks?

Anyone who's been writing long can attest that writing takes work. Some aspects are wonderful. We love creating characters and worlds. Some may even enjoy the process of throwing their characters into harrowing situations and watching them squirm and grow. Suspense writers, I'm looking at you. The creative process and a love of story prompted our journey as writers to begin.

While we may grumble when we accidentally write our characters into a corner they can't escape or whine about writer's block impeding the story, we love what we do. If we didn't, very few of us would find adequate inspiration to keep on when times get tough.

As much as we enjoy our work, there are tasks we may find less than appealing. Editing comes to mind. Or perhaps it's cover design or writing a blurb for your story. The thought of learning how to properly format your manuscript for print and eBook editions may make you break out in hives. And those are just the before-release tasks.

It could be the jobs you wish to avoid are related to publicity. You don't want the responsibility of setting up events, launch teams, or advertising. You're a writer, after all, not a publicist. Why should you have to learn how to do those things? A publisher can do them for you.

These types of thoughts could stem from pride, entitlement, or even laziness. Fear of failure or trepidation over learning new things could also prompt these ideas. Regardless of the driving force, you've come to believe traditional publishing is the only way to go.

Reasons to pursue one type of publishing over the other reflect possible attitude issues. While they may play a small part in your decision, if they bear a majority of the weight, it might be time to slow down. Ask God to search your heart and reveal any poor attitudes you may hold. God's wisdom is there for those who ask and having His wisdom guiding us is an important step in any decision-making process.

The remaining questions from our original list highlight some of the more valid reasons to pursue one type of publishing over another. Their answers can shed light on the path that's right for you.

A word of caution, though. If you feel God is clearly directing you down a particular path, even if the answers would tell you the other way is better, take the path God gives. Your journey may take longer. It may be more difficult. Or it could be filled with God's miraculous provision. Whatever the case, God's path is always the best path for you.

*What kind of budget is available?*

When I finished writing my first book, *Faith's Journey*, I mistakenly thought I'd finished the hard part of my publishing journey. Little did I know, story creation was going to be the least of my worries. Now, I had to figure out how to release my book into the world.

I'd attended enough writer's conferences to understand that I had two basic paths: indie publishing and traditional publishing. I prayed about it, and I felt God nudge me toward traditional publication.

Honoring God by putting out a book of quality, which would, in turn, help protect the integrity of Christian publishing, has always been important to me. Could I indie publish and accomplish this?

In theory, yes. But theory and reality were at odds in my world. With four school-age children at home, my minimum wage job wouldn't provide what I needed monetarily to produce a quality book. Short of miraculous provision, I could not afford a cover designer, editor, or someone to format the manuscript.

I did my research on both traditional and indie publishing. I knew the costs I faced if I chose indie publishing. God could provide, and I believed that wholeheartedly. But as I prayed, I didn't sense Him guiding me down that path.

Instead, I felt the nudge to seek traditional publication. I prayed over the publishers to query, knowing that prayer did not guarantee one of them would say yes. I researched how to write a professional proposal and did my best to emulate what I found. Then, based on what I'd found in *The Christian Writer's Market Guide*, I mailed my queries and proposals out to a few publishers who accepted first-time authors.

For me, budget played a large role in my decision to seek traditional publication. Without the publisher believing in my story enough to take on the costs to see my work in print, *Faith's Journey* might not be published even now.

Looking at the cost to produce a publisher-quality book and defining your allowed budget can help determine your path. Remember, budget is only one factor, and it should never supersede what God tells you to do. However, an honest appraisal of what you have available and what you need is part of being a good steward of the gifts God gives.

Some may be shaking their heads. "But Heather," they say. "I published without all the expense. Why do I need an editor when I have Pro Writing Aid (or Grammarly or AutoCrit or some other editing tool)? Why do I need a cover designer when I can use a template from one of those free sites? Why do I need someone to format my book when I've already arranged it in chapters according to industry standards?"

The naysayers may be correct. It is possible to release a quality book in this manner. However, I would caution you to take care. I've seen well-meaning writers approach publication this way and end up with books that announced they were self-published the moment they are seen on a shelf or in a browser.

I have read some wonderful, strong, indie-published books. I'm proud to have these books on the shelves in my home and to have reviewed them on my blog. These authors took care to do what was necessary to make their books rise above the rest. But I've also seen many and read a few that were indie-published with less-than-stellar results.

## How technologically proficient are you?

Though not a deal breaker, this is another important consideration in determining your publishing direction. At the very least, every writer should have a working knowledge of Microsoft Word, including the track changes feature, as well as proficiency with your email program. Though there are many beneficial programs available, most publishers correspond via email and work in Microsoft Word for editing purposes. Knowing these programs helps show you are professional and capable.

If you're considering indie publishing and plan to complete most of the work yourself, you'll need familiarity with a few additional programs. Editing software, a program like Adobe Photoshop for cover design, and one such as Adobe InDesign or Vellum (or Atticus for PC users) for proper formatting are some of the basics.

If you're not proficient in using these, you can learn. Or, as mentioned earlier, you can outsource some of the needed tasks. For those who find that even after classes, they are technologically challenged, do-it-yourself indie publishing may not be the best option. Due to marketing needs, traditionally published authors may still find learning new programs beneficial, but the production of the manuscript itself doesn't require more than Microsoft Word.

Whether seeking traditional publication or indie publishing, there are options within the options. Navigating these unfamiliar choices can be daunting and discouraging. We want to make God's best choice for us. We desire to be good stewards of this gift He's given us. And we want our decisions as well as the finished product to honor Him.

In traditional publishing, there are a few large presses in the Christian market. Several of these are now owned by mainstream publishers, but the books they release are listed under the Christian imprint. Most of these large publishing houses only accept manuscripts sent through agents. Read that again. They *only* accept agented submissions. It's a *requirement*—not a request or preference.

This means if you have your heart set on publishing with one of the big publishing houses, you'll either need to meet one of the editors at a conference and impress them with your story or find yourself an agent. This requires research into which agents are the best fit for you and your story. Instead of querying the publisher, you'll query the agent and wait for acceptance or rejection. And it's always good to remember that acquiring an agent doesn't guarantee your book will be picked up by a publisher.

The other traditional option is seeking publication with a small- to-medium-size press, which may also be referred to as indie publishing within the industry because they are independent from the large publishing conglomerates. The current *Christian Writer's Market Guide* is a valuable resource for both researching agents and smaller publishers. Not only will this book give insight into what each press is looking for and who to contact, but you can also find information on how many books are acquired from first-time authors.

Some of these publishing houses prefer manuscripts submitted through agents, but there are those that accept unsolicited manuscripts from authors. This information can be found in the guide or on the publisher's website. Ignoring the clear requests of a publisher is a quick way to take your finished manuscript from the slush pile to the rejection pile. Always follow each publisher's guidelines.

Those choosing the self-publishing route have even more possibilities. We've already covered doing everything yourself and hiring out individual tasks. Outside of those are vanity presses, hybrid publishers, and self-publishing assist programs.

Let's look at self-publishing assistance programs. There are a variety of programs available to help walk an author who wants to self-publish through the process. They offer the author a place to easily find the paid professional help they need to self-publish their book. However, the author is the one ultimately responsible for the publishing and marketing of their book.

The author using these services retains complete creative and financial control of their finished book. Quality control is also the author's responsibility. Not all self-publishing assistance programs are created equal. When considering a company to become your one-stop-shop for self-publishing needs, research is your friend. Examine the covers and editing of other books they've assisted in publication. Check out their ratings and even research if the books they've helped receive awards.

Like self-publishing assistance programs, hybrid and vanity publishing also offer everything you need to publish in one place. However, as with indie publishing, there are multiple ways to use the term "hybrid publishing"; for this discussion, we use it to refer to publishers who offer both traditional and self-publishing assistance. Whether self-publishing assistance services are offered by a publisher that also traditionally publishes or not, both this style and vanity press publishing require payment for services rendered. Each one results in a published book. Though they may appear closely related, the differences are a key factor.

Vanity presses typically do not vet their books. If you've put some words on a page, congratulations, you're accepted. Pay the company's fees, and they will put your book into print. Of course, there are always services you can add on to make your book even better, and they'll be happy to add that to your invoice.

While some authors using a vanity press retain the rights to their books, that is not always the case. Read the contract before agreeing to anything. These companies are not held to an industry standard in their work. Often, book covers are less than ideal and the pages are riddled with editing errors because they are typically published "as is." While the author may keep all profits from books sold, they've paid a high price for services and often must commit to buying a set number of books.

I've seen many authors on social media claiming they were scammed by programs like these. At times, upon closer inspection, I've found this is the result of authors eager to see their work in print.

Their excitement over the possibility of publication makes them quick to jump on the idea that someone wants their book. I would caution you not to allow your eagerness to make you prey for predatory companies.

As with independent and hybrid self-publishing assistance programs, careful research about vanity publishers is your friend. Check out any company offering a deal that sounds too good to be true. If they promise certain sales levels or even brag about how many sales their authors typically see, that's a red flag. Also, check out the quality of the books they've helped publish. Read one or two. Find company reviews online.

The time between writing and publishing a book can be exciting and daunting and frustrating. The wait can seem indefinite, maybe even eternal. But it's not.

Remember, God is in control of your publishing journey. Don't let impatience push you into places He never intended you to go. What you learn in those places often means unnecessary pain and setbacks as you move back into what God wanted for you all along.

Even those authors who want to avoid vanity presses can fall into the trap of unscrupulous companies. There are times when vanity presses present themselves as hybrid publishing companies, making it even more difficult for new authors to avoid them.

You know what I'm going to say here. The way to avoid being taken advantage of by a vanity press in a hybrid press's clothing is through knowledge and research.

Even those who have been writing and publishing for a while can find all these definitions and cautions confusing and overwhelming. You are not alone. We've all had to determine God's best path for our publishing journeys. And our starting path may not be our final path.

Whether traditional, agented, one of the methods of indie publishing, or hybrid publishing seems to be your best path, cover your decisions in prayer. Be open to the experiences of others who have walked the road before you. While their journey may not be the same one God has for you, we can still learn from each other and help each other find publishing success.

ACTION STEP

Slow down. Revisit the types of publishing options available to you. Were there any you felt an immediate *no* about? Was it caution or pride creating the feeling? Sometimes, it helps to write down your options, along with the pros and cons of each one. Take the time to do that. Now, with your list in front of you, start praying about the choices. Ask Him to give you wisdom and guide you in His best path for you. Ask God for clarity about which paths you should definitely stay away from. As He speaks to your heart, mark off those things from your list, even if they looked good at first. If you end up with more than one option, continue your research about them and what is necessary for publication in each one.

# 13

# MOVING FORWARD

Have you ever noticed the crazy expectations we place on high school graduation? Just listen to some of the valedictory speeches. Unbridled optimism about how the graduates are moving from childhood into adulthood. They're saying goodbye to what came before and moving into this wonderful land of opportunity as adults.

Sure, most will mention initial trepidation, but almost everyone quickly veers into the preparation time they've completed and how they know they're ready for what's to come. The promise of success is spread before them like a banquet, waiting for them to snatch it up.

Then reality hits. College is harder than expected. Maybe they didn't have as much practice balancing work and family and school and social life as they imagined. Those dreams they dreamed in vivid color fade to black and white as they lose sight of what they were most passionate about amid the demands of living as adults.

Adulting is hard, and it isn't always as fun as we thought it would be.

The writing journey is no different. So, here is your writing valedictorian address.

> Congratulations. You've done it! You have stepped into the world of writing. You've read craft books, attended workshops, and listened to podcasts. Whether you're writing full-time or have a day job to pay the bills, you're ready to join the ranks as an author.
>
> You've moved from thinking about that nagging story idea to putting the words on paper. That alone is more than most accomplish. And finishing the manuscript? Be proud of your hard work. You're in the top three percent for reaching the end. Most writers abandon their stories long before they're complete.
>
> Celebrate your accomplishment. But be prepared. The life of an author can be confusing and frustrating at times. Everyone who's anyone will tell you their way is the way to stronger writing and success in publication. Yet, their methods or programs rub you raw like ill-fitting shoes. Periods of discouragement may suck the joy from the journey. Some of those times may even make you question your sanity in choosing the writer's path.
>
> Don't quit. As Joshua commanded the Israelites in scripture, be strong and courageous. You've felt God's nudge toward writing. You've given Him this dream, and He's entrusted it back to you. Cover your path with prayer and stand firm in your calling. God equips those He has called.

 *Cover your path with prayer and stand firm in your calling. God equips those He has called.*

When your mind is reeling with all the should-do's and must-do's of writing, remember two things: First, your journey is your own. Find out who God created you to be as a person and a writer. Second, inside every rule, program, and method for writing, there is a purpose. Use your teachable heart to find that purpose and honor it in the ways that fit the unique writer God created you to be.

When you blend the heart of the writing rules with practices that are a natural fit for your personality, the writer inside is freed to experience more productivity and greater excellence in storytelling. You are prepared. Keep going. You write you.

# ADDITIONAL RESOURCES

From methods and writing craft books to programs designed for writers, these tools can help you write with excellence in ways that honor the writer God created you to be. I pray you find them useful in your writing journey. But remember, some of these materials are not written from a Christian perspective. Be selective about which ones you choose to use.

**Online Project Planner and Progress Trackers**

- Livingwriter.com
- Scrivener
- Storyist.com
- WriteTrack.cloud

**Books about the Publishing Industry and Process**

- *Getting Past the Publishing Gatekeepers* by Hope Bollinger, Linda Fulkerson, Rowena Kuo, and Carrie Schmidt

*Additional Resources*

- *The Christian Writer's Market Guide* by Steve Laube

**Books on Plot**

- *How to Write a Brilliant Romance* by Susan May Warren
- *Romancing the Beat: Story Structure for Romance Novels (How to Write Kissing Books)* by Gwen Hayes
- *Save the Cat* by Blake Snyder
- *Save the Cat Writes a Novel* by Jessica Brody
- *The Story Equation* by Susan May Warren

**Other Plotting Methods to Investigate**

- 27 Chapter Method—Kat O'Keefe
- The Hero's Journey—based on Joseph Campbell's *The Hero with a Thousand Faces*
- The Plot Dot—Derek Murphy
- The Story Circle—Dan Harmon

**Books on Character**

- *Exploring the Art of Character* by DiAnn Mills
- *Getting into Character* by Brandilyn Collins
- *GMC: Goal Motivation & Conflict* by Debra Dixon
- *How to Write Dazzling Dialogue* by James Scott Bell
- *Plot Versus Character: A Balanced Approach to Writing Great Fiction* by Jeff Gerke
- *The Dance of Character and Plot* by DiAnn Mills
- *Writing Unforgettable Characters: How to Create Story People Who Jump Off the Page* by James Scott Bell

# ACKNOWLEDGMENTS

Listing everyone who has influenced my writing journey is impossible. I've sat under so many wonderful, knowledgeable teachers through conferences, books, podcasts, and personal interactions. Each one has helped me grow, and I would not be the author I am today without them.

There are two, however, I have to mention by name.

Kristen Heitzmann has long been the author I look to when I consider the quality of writing I aspire to. More than inspiration, she is also the first author who gave me permission to embrace my natural tendencies in writing without feeling like they doomed me to failure.

Many have encouraged and strengthened my understanding of God-designed personalities. None so much as Linda Goldfarb. From the first workshop of hers I attended to the intensive training in the LINKED® Personality System and the friendship we've developed since, she has encouraged my interest in understanding and accepting myself as God created me, in both my personal and writing life.

# ABOUT THE AUTHOR

Heather Greer is a preacher's kid and pastor's wife who loves using her passion for reading and writing to encourage others in their faith. She has been a finalist for the Selah Awards twice. In addition to all things book-related, Heather loves baking. Christmas baking is her favorite, and each year, she makes dozens of treats to pass on to her family and friends in southern Illinois. And while it isn't her favorite, she's even been known to add gingerbread people to her cookie trays.

# OTHER WRITING CRAFT BOOKS YOU MAY LIKE

*Magic Words: How to Enchant Judges & Conjure Contest Wins*

*by Ellen E. Withers*

Transform your book, short fiction, or nonfiction work into a spellbinding, prize-worthy contest winner with Magic Words: How to Enchant Judges and Conjure Contest Wins. When you apply the magic found inside, you'll produce bewitching tales that will charm readers and contest judges.

Have you wondered what a contest judge really cares about when judging a contest?

Magic Words provides the information every writer needs to craft prizewinning contest entries for novels, short fiction, and nonfiction work. It's a tremendous resource that disseminates the techniques judges want to see in contest submissions, as well as contest-winning tips and opinions from multiple contest judges.

Written by a multiple prize-winning author who has judged multitudes of writing contests, Magic Words has the answers for you. Packed with opinions and suggestions from twelve contest judges, this guide shares what you need to win. When you apply the recommended skills to your contest entries, your work will bewitch judges and conjure an enchanting contest winner.

Get your copy here:

https://scrivenings.link/magicwords

\* \* \*

***Getting Past the Publishing Gatekeepers: Winning the Hearts of Agents, Publishers, Editors, and Readers***

There are four "gatekeepers" in publishing: Agents, publishers, editors, and readers. So how do authors win their hearts?

**Agents**

Love 'em or hate 'em, agents are a necessity in the publishing industry. Former agent Hope Bolinger will walk you through what makes a good agent, how to win them over, and how to break up with a bad agent.

**Publishers**

Becoming a published author can be one of the most exciting and rewarding events in your life. However, understanding (and enduring) the publication process can be one of the most frightening and frustrating. Publisher Linda

Fulkerson offers tips and tidbits that can help alleviate your angst and bypass the bafflements.

**Editors**

On the road to publication, editors can be your greatest challenges and your best friends. This section focuses on how editing before submission can better prepare your manuscript for presentation to publishers and what you can expect from editors throughout the life of your work. Rowena Kuo shares how to create that masterpiece manuscript that can navigate through the publishing process, pre-contract to post-publication.

**Readers**

Once all the other gates have been opened, the author must now win the hearts of readers. Influencer Carrie Schmidt offers practical tips and behind-the-scenes insights that will show you the path to getting your book in front of new readers—and keeping them for the long haul. Your story matters. Here's how to get it read.

Get your copy here:
https://scrivenings.link/gatekeepers

\* \* \*

*Stay up-to-date on your favorite books and authors with our free e-newsletters.*

ScriveningsPress.com

# ALSO BY HEATHER GREER

### From the Stained-glass Legacy collection:

*Window of Opportunity*

Faith and duty drive Evangeline Moore to protect her father's pristine image as a judge in Harrisburg, Illinois. Her resolve's biggest test? Dot, her childhood friend. With Evangeline beside her, Dot's desire for the Roaring Twenties' glitz and glamor leads the pair into questionable situations.

Born into a Chicago mob family, Brendan Dunne understands duty, but faith puts him at odds with his father's demands. Even when his brother James's propensity for trouble lands them in Harrisburg, the truth is undeniable. To their father, the lines he won't cross mean Brendan will never measure up.

When circumstances push Brendan and Evangeline together, unexpected events create an opportunity to break free of family expectations. Will they be brave enough to forge their own path before the window closes on their chance to change?

Get your copy here:
https://scrivenings.link/windowofopportunity

## Stand-alone Novels (Contemporary Romance)

*Love in the Squared Circle*
by **Heather Greer**

Trinity Knight is not a fan of professional wrestling. But with her husband gone, it falls to her to give their son the father-son trip they daydreamed about when he was alive. After Trinity causes them to miss a meet and greet with Jay's favorite wrestler, a random act of kindness saves the trip and starts Trinity on an unexpected path.

Universal Wrestling Organization Champion Blane Sterling hears whiny children at photo ops all the time. However, overhearing a young boy comfort his mother piques his interest. Touched by their story, Blane works with the UWO Public Relations team to give Jay the experience of a lifetime.

As they learn each other's stories, Trinity and Blane are drawn to each other. But they don't just come from different states. They live in different worlds. Trinity might learn to fit into his life, but can those in her world look beyond Blane's profession to see his heart? Or will a lack of acceptance cause Trinity and Blane to lose their shot at love?

Get your copy here:
https://scrivenings.link/loveinthesquaredcircle

***Cake That!***

Competing on the *Cake That* baking show is a dream come true for Livvy Miller, but debt on her cupcake truck and an expensive repair make her question if it's one she should chase. Her best friend, Tabitha, encourages Livvy to trust God to care for The Sugar Cube, win or lose.

Family is everything to Evan Jones. His parents always gave up their dreams so their children could achieve theirs. Winning *Cake That* would let him give back some of what they've sacrificed by allowing him to give them the trip they've always talked about but could never afford.

As the contestants live and bake together, more than the competition heats up. Livvy and Evan have a spark from the start, but they're in it to win. Neither needs the distraction of romance. Unwanted attention from Will, another competitor, complicates matters. Stir in strange occurrences to the daily baking assignments, and everyone wonders if a saboteur is in the mix.

With the distractions inside and outside the *Cake That* kitchen, will Livvy or Evan rise above the rest and claim the prize? Or does God have more in store for them than they first imagined?

Get your copy here:

scrivenings.link/cakethat

## Novella Collections:

***Pets Amore***

*A novella collection—including "Pegboards, Parrots, and Pickup Lines" by Heather Greer*

**Pegboards, Parrots, and Pickup Lines**—Charlotte Herring wants one thing—to prove she can succeed on her own. But to avoid failure, she needs the people of Brookview to accept her and her antique store. For years, Tyson Abbott's only goal was to realize his father's dreams for the family hardware store. After meeting the town's newest resident, he adds a new goal—helping Charlotte find her place in Brookview.

With a parrot named Cracker Jack paving the way for their partnership to become a romance, Charlotte and Tyson see more than the dreams for their stores coming true. But when their plans conflict and past hurts resurface, will they lose their dreams and each other?

Get your copy here:
https://scrivenings.link/petsamore

## A Match Made at Christmas

*A novella collection—including "The Santa Setup"*

*by Heather Greer*

**The Santa Setup**—Turning friendship into love takes magic. Good thing Nicholas Eckert and Julie Clarke work at Christmas Wonderland. The attraction brims with holiday magic, not to mention four teenage elves determined that Mr. and Mrs. Claus stop playing a couple and become one. The teens will need more than mistletoe to pair up these two. Julie is seeing someone, and Nick won't risk their friendship for possible love. Only the elven employees' outrageous antics stand a chance of setting up Santa in time for Christmas.

Get your copy here:

https://scrivenings.link/amatchmadeatchristmas

**Love Delivered**

*A novella collection—including "Sweet Delivery"*

*by Heather Greer*

**Sweet Delivery**—After winning Cake That, Will Forrester thinks his Pastry Perfect Baking Dreams have come true. The sweetness fades when a chain bakery moves to town, and Will must adjust his plans to keep his customers. Hiring Erica Gerard is one of those changes. As they work together, Erica challenges Will and offers new ideas to improve the bakery. Soon, Erica and Will start bringing out the best in each other. But Erica harbors a secret, and if it's discovered, Will might never be the same.

Get your copy here:

https://scrivenings.link/lovedelivered

**Love in Any Season**

A novella collection—including "Sweet Delivery"

by Heather Greer

**Sugar and Spice**

Emeline Becker, owner of Sugar and Spice Bakery, loves New Kuchenbrünn, except for the gingerbread. As the only bakery, she supplies the annual Gingerbread Festival with the one treat she can't stand. It's gingerbread everywhere.

Things get worse when Ryker Lehmann is hired as the festival photographer. He was her secret teen crush, her sister's boyfriend, and witness to her worst humiliation. Plus, he broke her sister's heart and bruised hers when he left town after graduation. Now, he's back in town, determined to fix their friendship before the festival ends.

With gingerbread and Ryker together, can Emmie make it through the festival with her mind and heart intact?

Get your copy here:

https://scrivenings.link/loveinanyseason

\* \* \*

**Faith, Hope, and Love Series:**

*Faith's Journey*

**Faith, Hope, and Love Series - Book One**

https://scrivenings.link/faithsjourney

*Grasping Hope*

**Faith, Hope, and Love Series - Book Two**

https://scrivenings.link/graspinghope

*Relentless Love*

**Faith, Hope, and Love Series - Book Three**

https://scrivenings.link/relentlesslove

www.ingramcontent.com/pod-product-compliance
Lightning Source LLC
Chambersburg PA
CBHW071717020426
42333CB00017B/2297